THE

Jane Austen

MISCELLANY

THE
Jane Austen
MISCELLANY

LAUREN NIXON

First published 2012

The History Press
The Mill, Brimscombe Port
Stroud, Gloucestershire, GL5 2QG
www.thehistorypress.co.uk

British Library Cataloguing in Publication Data.
A catalogue record for this book is available from the British Library.

ISBN 978 0 7524 6863 1

Typesetting and origination by The History Press
Printed in Great Britain
Manufacturing managed by Jellyfish Print Solutions Ltd

· CONTENTS ·

· INTRODUCTION ·

Of personal attractions she possessed a considerable share. Her stature was that of true elegance. It could not have been increased without exceeding the middle height. Her carriage and deportment were quiet, yet graceful. Her features were separately good. Their assemblage produced an unrivalled expression of that cheerfulness, sensibility, and benevolence, which were her real characteristics. Her complexion was of the finest texture. It might with truth be said, that her eloquent blood spoke through her modest cheek. Her voice was extremely sweet. She delivered herself with fluency and precision. Indeed she was formed for elegant and rational society, excelling in conversation as much as in composition.

Henry Austen, 'Biographical Notice of the Author'

In person she was very attractive; her figure was rather tall and slender, her step light and firm, and her whole appearance expressive of health and animation. In complexion she was a clear brunette with a rich colour; she had full

round cheeks, with mouth and nose small and well formed
bright hazel eyes, and brown hair forming natural curls
close round her face.

James Edward Austen Leigh

Mama says she was then the prettiest, silliest, most
affected, husband-hunting butterfly she ever remembers
... [but by 1815] she was no more regarded in society than
a poker or a fire screen or any other thin, upright piece of
wood or iron that fills its corner in peace and quiet. The
case is very different now; she is still a poker, but a poker
of whom everyone is afraid.

Mary Russell Mitford

Who was Jane Austen? It's a question with a more com-
plicated answer than you might imagine. Since her first
publication in 1811, Austen has gone from total ano-
nymity to a literary saint to the queen of romance. Her
physical appearance is still something of a mystery, with a
small unfinished and unflattering sketch done by her sister
Cassandra being the only definite likeness. There is another
watercolour done by her sister in which Jane, dressed in a
blue bonnet and pelisse, faces away into the distance, and a
small painting in James Stanier Clarke's 'Friendship Book'
labelled as Jane Austen, but neither give much indication
to her features. Unlike the writers who Austen enjoyed and
admired, such as Samuel Johnson and Fanny Burney, she was
no celebrity, staying out of the public eye by keeping her
authorship a secret.

Austen was born on 16 December 1775 to the Reverend George and Mrs Cassandra Austen during a particularly cold winter, and for the first twenty-five years of her life home

A coloured engraving based on the Cassandra portrait. (*c.* 1873)

would be the Rectory at Steventon, Hampshire. In 1801 Jane's
father made the decision to retire, moving his wife and daughters to Bath, a place Jane neither admired nor enjoyed. After
five years, four homes and the tragic death of Mr Austen, the
Austen women stayed a few years at Southampton before settling at Chawton Cottage in 1809. Having written her whole
life, Jane would redraft the novels of her youth – *Sense and
Sensibility*, *Pride and Prejudice* and *Northanger Abbey* – and pen
three more, *Mansfield Park*, *Emma* and *Persuasion*. Since her first
publication in 1811 Jane Austen has gone from an anonymous
success to Victorian ideal to the godmother of modern chick-
lit. Yet, like the few scarce images available of Austen, none of
these seems to feel quite right. Her letters reveal a woman
with a keen eye for fashion and society, a sharp, witty tongue
and a genuine liveliness of nature who could never have suited
the strict morality of the Victorian period. Though her novel's
love stories are significant contributors to her continuing
success, Austen was too much of a social satirist to really be
considered 'chick-lit'.

So what was Jane Austen? She was the daughter of a country clergyman, a young lady who enjoyed dancing and society,
who travelled often but never left the south of England. She
was a devoted sister and later aunt, with a passion for reading
and talent with a pen. She never married, and in her lifetime
refused any celebrity. Despite the sturdiness of her siblings,
Jane was struck by an illness still speculated about today and
died in Winchester on 18 July 1817, aged 41.

Many of Jane Austen's letters were destroyed after her
death, first by her sister Cassandra and later by various

nieces and nephews. For a twenty-first-century Austen fan the loss of such important documents is tragic; we lament what insight they could have held, what mysteries they could have solved. Whilst the surviving letters are invaluable in our understanding of Austen's life and person, the silences in between them are tantalising. What occurred there that Cassandra thought necessary to destroy the evidence? Of course, the absence of these letters hasn't stopped critics from speculating; they scour the remaining letters, as well as those of her friends and family, for some indication of a love affair or scandal. We cannot leave Austen alone, and the lack of material only continues to fuel our curiosity. It doesn't help perhaps that the lives

The proud but handsome Mr Darcy. (*Pride and Prejudice*, Hugh Thomson)

of her family are so varied and interesting. What wonderful, vibrant people they seem. There are soldiers and sailors, wealthy gentleman and aristocratic connections, as well as other brilliant literary minds. The Austen family anecdotes are almost as entertaining as Jane's novels, and they serve as a pleasing insight into her inspirations and motives.

But for her life to be picked apart and analysed never was Austen's intention. She preferred to keep her identity as the anonymous Lady responsible for *Pride and Prejudice* on a need-to-know basis, and watched and listened with amusement to what society had to say. For Austen, the words she placed on paper were the most important thing. That's why each section of this book is filled with quotes from Austen's novels and her letters, because if you are looking for the real Jane Austen, you need look no further than the wisdom and witticisms of her pen.

MEN

THE FRENCH REVOLUTION, AND the subsequent fall of the French monarchy and aristocracy, had an immense impact on Regency England. For years English fashions had followed the trends set by the French courts, which at the time of the Revolution were presided over by King Louis XVI and his queen, the stylish Marie Antoinette. Women's fashion's mimicked the excessive, elaborate hooped dresses worn by the Queen of France and men's fashions were no less extravagant. Somewhat thanks to the practice of sending the well-to-do on the Grand Tour, which exposed them to European culture and influenced their ideas of fashionable dress, men's fashion had become almost effeminate. Their hair was worn long, styled elaborately and often tied at the back with ribbon, and finally powdered – though many at court chose to wear a wig. The staple of a Georgian gentleman's attire was the frockcoat, which was tightly fitted around the chest and flared from the waist. Like women's dresses, these coats were often made of intricate brocade and expensive materials, worn with breeches, white stockings and low-heeled shoes with large buckles. These fashions are worlds away from the much swooned over masculine styles worn by the likes of Colin Firth in screen adaptations of Jane Austen's novels, so what caused such a dramatic change?

When the Revolution began in 1789, it would put an end to the excess of the French aristocracy and change social ideals forever. However, it would also bring about the rise of Napoleon Bonaparte, the self-styled Emperor of the French, whose ambitions for power would drag Britain into a series of fierce wars. In France the fashions of Louis XVI's court went into quick decline, as to appear an aristocrat was to condemn oneself willingly to the guillotine. In England style suffered too; not only did fashionable society no longer have a French court from which to take its lead, it no longer had access to the materials. With England and France at war, trade between the two countries ground to a halt and English society was forced to look within its own borders for inspiration and materials. This spawned a dramatic change in both fashion and polite society, as without French competition the English trade was able to thrive and develop, resulting in a rapid expansion of the middle classes. Fortunes were made and titles were granted, propelling the families of merchants and tradesmen, like Mr Bingley's, into the ranks of polite society. There was suddenly a new generation of young men being given the education previously reserved only for the sons of the upper class, all anxious to be fashionable enough to earn a reputation and marry an accomplished (and hopefully wealthy) young lady to further

He carpentered.

Captain Wentworth's friend, Captain Harville. (*Persuasion*, Hugh Thomson)

their family's status. For these new generations, their trendsetters were not the French courtiers, but the brave young men of the army and navy.

As the Napoleonic Wars raged, military and naval officers in their handsome, fitted uniforms became quite the male ideal. Championed by Beau Brummell, a friend of the Prince Regent and something of a style icon, the Georgian suit was abandoned for a simpler, more masculine style inspired by military designs. Tailoring would be crucial to the Regency gentleman, as the silhouette was everything; the object of the new trend was an image of classical masculinity: powerful, lean and heroic. The frockcoat was replaced by the cut-away riding jacket, worn over a waistcoat and shirt with a high, well-tied and well-starched cravat. Breeches and stockings were swapped for tight-fitting, usually pale-coloured pantaloons worn with riding boots. The huge wigs and powdered hair styles of the Georgians were quickly forgotten too – partially because of an increased tax on hair powder – and men began to wear their hair in short curls, inspired by the manly, classical heroes of Greece and Rome. The tricorne hat began to lose its popularity to what would eventually become the top hat, somewhat due to its impracticality, but also because these tall hats complimented the desired silhouette and gave the illusion of height.

These are the men of Jane Austen's novels; gentlemen who hunt, ride and stride through the countryside whilst cutting an impressive figure. The fashion would be so popular

– and dare we say effective – that it remained relatively the same for almost a century. The new fashion also came with a new ideal of behaviour, one that Austen depicts quite perfectly in *Emma*'s Mr Knightley, as well as *Pride and Prejudice*'s Bingley and Darcy, and the heroes of the two 'Bath Novels', Mr Tilney and Captain Wentworth. The Regency gentleman was expected to adhere to a certain mode of behaviour and morals, almost in a return to the medieval notion of chivalry, and Austen's novels feature a number of debates about what constitutes 'gentlemanly' behaviour. Mr Knightley is the exemplary gentleman: he is elegant without arrogance, conscious of social expectations and codes without snobbery and manages his estate with good sense and generosity. Throughout *Emma* it is Mr Knightley whose judgement Austen encourages the reader to trust; he suspects an intimacy between Jane Fairfax and Frank Churchill that the rest of Highbury is blind to, as well as Mr Elton's designs on Emma. Darcy, though proud, is the saviour of both his sister's and Lydia Bennet's reputations and is ultimately allowed to be the exemplary gentleman he thinks himself. Captain Wentworth, meanwhile, is the proof that birth does not make a man a gentleman. He is gallant, intelligent and handsome, his behaviour chivalrous and his manner reserved without being rude. These are the sorts of men to whom Austen grants happy endings, who are deserving of her heroines' affections and will check her flaws.

Yet Austen's 'ungentlemanly' characters, such as Mr Wickham or Mr Willoughby, are painted so attractively! Of course the awfulness of their behaviour would not be half as effective if the reader did not share the infatuations of Elizabeth and Marianne. But still, there is a sense that Austen must have had something of a soft spot for these rogues to portray them so effectively. Jane was not entirely unfamiliar to such behaviour: her favourite brother Henry, an officer in

"Conjecturing as to the date"

Conjecturing to the date of Mr Bingley's return. (*Pride and Prejudice*, Hugh Thomson)

the militia, could perhaps have been the inspiration for Mr Wickham. Though certainly not as bad as Wickham, Henry was not always as well behaved as his sensible brothers. Despite her being married and ten years his senior, Henry shared a flirtatious relationship with the Austen's glamorous cousin, Eliza. Eliza and her mother, Mr Austen's sister Philadelphia Hancock, moved to Paris after her father's death, where Eliza enjoyed a lifestyle that included attending royal events and marrying a titled French army captain, the Comte Jean François Capot de Feuillide. Though Eliza, now the Comtesse de Feuillide, escaped the violence of the Revolution for the English shore, her husband was arrested and guillotined in 1794. The now single Eliza was then pursued by the newly widowed James Austen, as well as his younger brother, and though both were refused, Henry was undeterred. Jane's letters from September 1796 do show Henry engaged, but not to Eliza. His betrothed was a Miss Mary Pearson, and his intentions appear serious; a miniature of her was circulated within the family and Henry schemed to have her introduced at Steventon. Whether the visit took place is not recorded, but by 7 November the engagement was no more and Eliza wrote to her cousin Phylly Walter that:

Our Cousin Henry Austen has been in Town he looks thin & ill – I hear his late intended is a most intolerable Flirt, and reckoned to give herself great Airs – the person who mentioned this to me says She is a pretty wicked looking Girl with bright Black Eyes which pierce thro' & thro'. No wonder the poor young Man's heart could not withstand them.

Whether Henry was truly jilted is unclear; it could have been a plot to entice Eliza's jealousy and affections, as she finally accepted him the following year.

What of Jane herself? Were men ever to be anything but brothers, cousins and friends? Though Austen never married, her critics and admirers have always looked desperately for some form of romance. Though it is possible that any evidence of a serious attachment may have been burned by Cassandra after her sister's death, it seems that her strongest male relationships were those she shared with her brothers. However, this doesn't mean that Austen was entirely against being wooed, as her letters to Cassandra in January 1796 reveal. Though Jon Spence's *Becoming Jane*, and more so the 2007 film inspired by it, make much of Jane Austen's flirtation with Tom Lefroy, the reality is not quite so grand or romantic. Tom was the Irish nephew of the Lefroys of Ashe Rectory, the Austen's neighbours and Jane's particular friends, and his acquaintance with Jane lasted for little more than a month. Jane's behaviour seems to have been rather like Miss Marianne Dashwood's, and her letters imply that she was properly scolded by Cassandra for her openness. But by 17 January Tom was gone, apparently never to be mentioned again:

At length the day is come on which I am to flirt my last with Tom Lefroy, and when you receive this it will be over. My tears flow as I write at the melancholy idea.

Tom would go on to have a successful law career, serving as Lord Chief Justice of Ireland from 1852 until 1866. Though some theories have suggested that Jane's 'relationship' with

"Mr Darcy with him".

Mr Darcy and Mr Bingley return to Netherfield. (*Pride and Prejudice*, Hugh Thomson)

Tom inspired the first version of *Pride and Prejudice*, known as *First Impressions*, the connection is tenuous. Tom Lefroy was a poor law student who admired Henry Fielding's vivacious hero, the foundling Tom Jones, a little too much. Though their meeting and the novel's composition overlap, that he or Jane's affection for him could have inspired the wealthy, proud Fitzwilliam Darcy and his ardent, undeniable passion for Elizabeth Bennet is extremely unlikely.

They are the most conceited creatures in the world, and think themselves of so much importance!

Northanger Abbey

Stupid men are the only ones worth knowing, after all.

Pride and Prejudice

I assure you. I have no notion of treating men with such respect. That is the way to spoil them.

Northanger Abbey

We have just received a visit from Mr Tom Lefroy and his cousin George. The latter is really very well-behaved now; and as for the other, he has but *one* fault, which time will, I trust, entirely remove – it is that his morning coat is a great deal too light. He is a very great admirer of Tom Jones, and therefore wears the same coloured clothes.

Letter to Cassandra Austen, 9 January 1796

It is a truth universally acknowledged, that a single man in possession of a good fortune, must be in want of a wife.

Pride and Prejudice

There is one thing, Emma, which a man can always do if he chuses, and that is, his duty; not by manoeuvring and finessing, but by vigour and resolution.

Emma

Poor Edward! It is very hard that he who has everything else in the World that he can wish for, should not have good health too.

Letter to Cassandra Austen, 9 January 1799

Kitty and Lydia take his defection much more to heart than I do. They are young in the ways of the world, and not yet open to the mortifying conviction that handsome young men must have something to live on, as well as the plain.

Pride and Prejudice

It was now his object to marry. He was rich, and being turned on shore, fully intended to settle as soon as he could be properly tempted; actually looking round, ready to fall in love with all the speed which a clear head and a quick taste could allow. He had a heart for either of the Miss Musgroves, if they could catch it; a heart, in short, for any pleasing young woman who came in his way.

Persuasion

I cannot think well of a man who sports with any woman's feelings; and there may often be a great deal more suffered than a stander-by can judge.

Mansfield Park

Your amiable young man can be amiable only in French, not in English. He may be very 'aimable', have very good manners, and be very agreeable; but he can have no English delicacy towards the feelings of other people: nothing really amiable about him.

Emma

Such a change in a man of so much pride exciting not only astonishment but also gratitude — for to love, ardent love, it must be attributed; and as such its impression on her was a sort to be encouraged, as by no means unpleasing.

Pride and Prejudice

There is something wanting, his figure is not striking — it has none of that grace which I should expect in the man who could seriously attach my sister. His eyes want all that spirit, that fire, which at once announce virtue and intelligence.

Sense and Sensibility

I am an advocate for early marriages, where there are means in proportion, and would have every young man, with a sufficient income, settle as soon after four-and-twenty as he can.

Mansfield Park

Men of sense, whatever you may chuse to say, do not want silly wives.

Emma

He is such a disagreeable man, that it would be quite a misfortune to be liked by him.

Pride and Prejudice

A man does not recover from such a devotion of the heart to such a woman! He ought not; he does not.

Persuasion

A little less open-heartedness would have made him a higher character. – General benevolence, but not general friendship, made a man what ought to be.

Emma

Heaven forbid! *That* would be the greatest misfortune of all! – To find a man agreeable whom one is determined to hate! Do not wish me such an evil.

Pride and Prejudice

No man is offended by another man's admiration of the woman he loves, it is the woman only who can make it a torment.

Northanger Abbey

I am glad I have done being in love with him. I should not like a man who is so soon discomposed by a hot morning.

Emma

His person and air were equal to what her fancy had ever drawn for the hero of a favourite story; and in his carrying her into the house with so little previous formality, there was a rapidity of thought which particularly recommended the action to her. Every circumstance belonging to him was interesting. His name was good, his residence was in their favourite village, and she soon found out that of all manly dresses a shooting-jacket was the most becoming. Her imagination was busy, her reflections were pleasant, and the pain of a sprained ankle was disregarded.

Sense and Sensibility

We must not expect a lively young man to be always so guarded and circumspect. It is very often nothing but our own vanity that deceives us. Women fancy admiration means more than it does.

Pride and Prejudice

Men have had every advantage of us in telling their own story. Education has been theirs in so much higher a degree; the pen has been in their hands.

Persuasion

Man only can be aware of the insensibility of man towards a new gown.

Northanger Abbey

He is just what a young man ought be ... sensible, good-humoured, lively; and I never saw such happy manners! – so much ease, with such perfect good breeding!

Pride and Prejudice

A young man ... so easily falls in love with a pretty girl for a few weeks, and when accident separates them so easily forgets her, that these sort of inconstancies are very frequent.

Pride and Prejudice

His temper might perhaps be a little soured by finding, like many others of his sex, that through some unaccountable bias in favour of beauty, he was the husband of a very silly woman – but she knew that this kind of blunder was too common for any sensible man to be lastingly hurt by it.

Sense and Sensibility

One man's style must not be the rule of another's.

Emma

Is there such a Henry in the world who could be insensible to such a declaration? Henry Tilney at least was not.

Northanger Abbey

But perhaps you young ladies may not care about the beaux, and had as lief be without them as with them. For my part, I think they are vastly agreeable, provided they dress smart and behave civil. But I can't bear to see them dirty and nasty.

Sense and Sensibility

There certainly are not so many men of large fortune in the world as there are pretty women to deserve them.

Mansfield Park

Her thoughts were silently fixed on the irreparable injury which too early an independence and its consequent habits of idleness, dissipation, and luxury, had made in the mind, the character, the happiness, of a man who, to every advantage of person and talents, united a disposition naturally open and honest, and a feeling, affectionate temper. The world had made him extravagant and vain – Extravagance and vanity had made him cold-hearted and selfish.

Sense and Sensibility

He was just entering into life, full of spirits, and with all the liberal dispositions of an eldest son, who feels born only for expense and enjoyment.

Mansfield Park

A man would always wish to give a woman a better home than the one he takes her from; and he who can do it, where there is no doubt of her regard, must, I think, be the happiest of mortals.

Emma

He admires as a lover, not as a connoisseur. To satisfy me, those characters must be united. I could not be happy with a man whose taste did not in every point coincide with my own. He must enter into all my feelings; the same books, the same music must charm us both.

Sense and Sensibility

A man in distressed circumstances has not time for all those elegant decorums which other people may observe.

Pride and Prejudice

I give you all Joy of Frank's return, which happens in the true Sailor way, just after our being told not to expect him for some weeks.

Letter to Cassandra Austen, 30 June 1808

The navy, I think, who have done so much for us, have at least an equal claim with any other set of men, for all the comforts and all the privileges which any home can give. Sailors work hard enough for their comforts, we must all allow.

Persuasion

The profession, either navy or army, is its own justification. It has everything in its favour: heroism, danger, bustle, fashion. Soldiers and sailors are always acceptable in society. Nobody can wonder that men are soldiers and sailors.

Mansfield Park

Why are you like Queen Elizabeth? – Because you know how to chuse wise Ministers. – Does not this prove You as great a Captain as she was Queen?

Letter to Francis Austen, 3 July 1813

It is always incomprehensible to a man that a woman should ever refuse an offer of marriage.

Emma

There is a nobleness in the name of Edmund. It is a name of heroism and renown; of kings, princes and knights; and seems to breathe the spirit of chivalry and warm affections.

Mansfield Park

The more I know of the world, the more am I convinced that I shall never see a man whom I can really love. I require so much! He must have all Edward's virtues, and his person and manners must ornament his goodness with every possible charm.

Sense and Sensibility

Much, much impropriety! It has sunk him – I cannot say how it has sunk him in my opinion. So unlike what a man should be! None of the upright integrity, that strict adherence to truth and principle, that disdain of trick and littleness, which a man should display in every transaction of his life.

Emma

Had he been even old, ugly, and vulgar, the gratitude and kindness of Mrs. Dashwood would have been secured by any act of attention to her child; but the influence of youth, beauty, and elegance, gave an interest to the action which came home to her feelings.

Sense and Sensibility

He was the proudest, most disagreeable man in the world, and everybody hoped that he would never come there again.

Pride and Prejudice

It would be needless to say, that the gentlemen advanced in the good opinion of each other, as they advanced in each others acquaintance, for it could not be otherwise. Their resemblance in good principles and good sense, in disposition and manner of thinking, would probably have been sufficient to unite them in friendship, without any other attraction; but their being in love with two sisters, and two sisters fond of each other, made that mutual regard inevitable and immediate, which might otherwise have waited the effect of time and judgment.

Sense and Sensibility

A man who has been refused! How could I ever be foolish enough to expect a renewal of his love? Is there one among the sex, who would not protest against such a weakness as a second proposal to the same woman? There is no indignity so abhorrent to their feelings!

Pride and Prejudice

God forbid that I should undervalue the warm and faithful feelings of any of my fellow-creatures! I should deserve utter contempt if I dared to suppose that true attachment and constancy were known only by woman. No, I believe you capable of everything great and good in your married lives. I believe you equal to every important exertion, and to every domestic forbearance, so long as – if I may be allowed the expression, so long as you have an object. I mean while the woman you love lives, and lives for you. All the privilege I claim for my own sex (it is not a very enviable one: you need not covet it), is that of loving longest, when existence or when hope is gone!

Persuasion

· 2 ·

WOMEN

THE GROWTH IN THE middle classes caused by the aftermath of the French Revolution and the Napoleonic Wars was not only to affect the men of Regency England, but the women too. As English trade bloomed many a merchant found himself with the income to set his family up as landed gentry; houses could be purchased, sons sent to university and their daughters properly educated. Soon the daughters of tradesman could afford to be as accomplished and elegant as the daughters of baronets, and often in possession of a more substantial fortune. Like Sir Walter Elliot in *Persuasion*, many upper-class gentlemen had squandered their fortunes and so such girls became attractive prospects; one had title, the other money, and each would have desired the other's possession. However, such a dramatic shift in class system did not come without its confusions and Austen's novels betray a number of tensions.

In its disruption of the British class system, the Revolution had also shaken the country's social ideals. The liberal, left-wing policies of the new French Republic were beginning to be talked of on English shores and there were a number of small-scale riots. The values and morals of Georgian society were becoming increasingly at odds with the new Regency ones; as the fashions changed, so did people's attitudes. Women's dress had also become increasingly less extravagant

Harriet Smith is brought to
tears by Mr Elton's rejection.
(*Emma*, Chris Hammond)

"*The sight of Harriet's tears*"

since the Revolution, with the heavy, hooped skirts and restrictive corsets being abandoned for the classically inspired empire-line dresses. The intricately constructed, mammoth hairstyles fell out of favour too, with girls choosing to wear it in short curls at the front with their long hair tied up in a bun or woven with a ribbon or flowers for a ball – again inspired by images of Ancient Greece and Rome. This change in fashions may have been a superficial shift, but it was an important one; the freedom and simplicity of these trends was reflected in the ideals of those who wore it. With class boundaries no longer so strictly defined, what counted as good taste, breeding and manners became unclear and tensions began to rise between classes, sexes and generations.

The new more masculine fashions for men had created a new ideal for the Regency man to follow if he wished to be considered a gentleman; he was to be well mannered, chivalrous and strong. Both countryside pursuits and polite society were to be enjoyed without being indulged, much as he was expected to dress well without being foppish. But what of women? Austen's novels are full of conflicting views on how a lady should dress and behave, on what constituted being 'accomplished' and how independent and intelligent a girl might be permitted to be. Though Austen warns against marrying on brief acquaintances, as well as the dangers of taking a silly wife, it seems her opinions were not universal. In *Pride and Prejudice* the Miss Bennets are appalled when Mr Collins selects Dr James Fordyce's *Sermons to Young Women* (1766) to read to them. These sermons were part of a trend known as conduct literature: texts written to inform and instruct young

"*Marianne came hastily out of the parlour apparently in violent affliction*"

Marianne is left distraught after Mr Willoughby's sudden departure. (*Sense and Sensibility*, Chris Hammond)

ladies how to behave properly. Fordyce's opinions, such as 'Providence designed women for a state of dependence, and consequently of submission', would have been abhorrent to a girl like Elizabeth Bennet. Though the sermons were published before Jane Austen was born, her reference to them suggests that Fordyce's ideas were not wholly forgotten. One of the text's central ideas was that clever, witty women do not make good wives:

> Men who understand the science of domestic happiness, know that it's very first principle is ease. Of that indeed we grow fonder, in whatever condition, as we advance in life, and as the heat of youth abates. But we cannot be easy, where we are not safe. We are never safe in the company of a critic; and almost every wit is a critic by profession. In such company we are not at liberty to unbend ourselves. All must be the straining of study, or the anxiety of apprehension: how painful! Where the heart may not expand and open itself with freedom, farewell to real friendship, farewell to convivial delight! But to suffer this restraint at home, what misery! From the brandishing's of wit in the hand of ill nature, of imperious passion, or of unbounded vanity, who would not flee!

No wonder the Bennet girls were aghast at having to listen to such a book being read.

Pride and Prejudice in particular explores the tensions and conflicts surrounding Regency women by playing off characters with opposing beliefs and status against one another. There is Elizabeth Bennet, the poor but spirited, clever daughter of a gentleman; Caroline Bingley, the wealthy, fashionable daughter of self-made tradesmen; and Lady Catherine de Bourgh, the daughter of an earl. Whilst Elizabeth judges the other two for their character, she is judged by them on a far more superficial level. Caroline Bingley is part of the new set, a wealthy young woman eager to legitimise her status by marrying a man like Mr Darcy, which is why her snobbery is ugly and hypocritical. Unlike Emma Woodhouse, who is forgiven for snobbish ways, Caroline lacks the breeding to justify her criticisms of Elizabeth and the rest of society. Much of her judgement is based on appearance; for Caroline a lady who is not fashionable, elegant and refined is no lady at all:

Miss Bingley began abusing [Elizabeth] as soon as she was out of the room. Her manners were pronounced to be very bad indeed, a mixture of pride and impertinence; she had no conversation, no stile, no taste, no beauty. Mrs Hurst thought the same, and added,

'She has nothing, in short, to recommend her, but being an excellent walker. I shall never forget her appearance this morning. She really looked almost wild.'

'She did indeed, Louisa. I could hardly keep my countenance. Very nonsensical to come at all! Why must she be scampering about the country, because her sister had a cold? Her hair so untidy, so blowsy!'

'Yes, and her petticoat; I hope you saw her petticoat, six inches deep in mud, I am absolutely certain; and the gown which had been let down to hide it not doing its office.'

Lady Catherine's concepts of society and propriety, meanwhile, are informed by the values of the previous generation and seem antiquated when compared with the behaviour and opinions of the novel's youthful society. She deems Elizabeth unworthy of Mr Darcy predominantly due to what she perceives as her inferior birth. Elizabeth may be a gentleman's daughter, but to Lady Catherine her lack of connections makes her a wholly unsuitable candidate for mistress of Pemberley:

My daughter and my nephew are formed for each other. They are descended, on the maternal side, from the same noble line; and, on the father's, from respectable, honourable, and ancient – though untitled – families. Their fortune on both sides is splendid. They are destined for each other by the voice of every member of their respective houses; and what is to divide them? The upstart pretensions of a young woman without family, connections, or fortune.

Then, of course, there is Elizabeth Bennet: her judgements and opinions are formed on the sincerity of a person's manners and character. Amongst all of the conflicting ideas of what a woman should be it is Elizabeth who marries one of the most desired men in literary history. She may lack enough status of birth to be considered worthy by Lady Catherine de Bourgh or enough fashion in her person and manners to suit

Caroline Bingley, but it is her independent nature and lively mind that catches his affections:

> The fact is, that you were sick of civility, of deference, of officious attention. You were disgusted with the women who were always speaking and looking and thinking for *your* approbation alone. I roused and interested you, because I was so unlike *them*.

If Mr Darcy was not 'disgusted' with a woman who behaved only to suit or catch a man, then Jane Austen certainly was. *Northanger Abbey*'s Isabella Thorpe and *Sense and Sensibility*'s Lucy Steele both fit Elizabeth's description; their manners are entirely styled to seduce and their sweetness is eventually revealed to be little more than an act. Though her society might have been conflicted when it came to women, Austen's condemnation of the shallow snobs and dishonest husband hunters in favour of her honest, intelligent heroines reveals exactly what she believed a girl should be.

However, for all this, women in the Regency were still almost completely dependent on men. Only those with the wealth and independence of Emma Woodhouse could afford to remain both single and comfortable. Whilst their brothers could pursue careers and increase their fortunes, the only work proper for a middle- or upper-class lady to pursue must be preceded by the words 'needle' or 'charity'. The

He attended to her large, fat sighings.

Wentworth's speaks with Mrs Musgrove, as Anne listens, full of emotion. (*Persuasion*, Hugh Thomson)

only acceptable career for a young lady was as a governess, or perhaps a school teacher. Education was an increasingly important part of a young lady's upbringing, and her teachers would require a high level of accomplishment themselves. Though governesses and schools are mentioned in Austen's other novels, they are a particular concern of *Emma*: Mrs Weston is Emma's former governess, a career Jane Fairfax considers inevitable as an orphan with no fortune. Mrs Elton, having heard of Mrs Weston's former employment, is 'rather astonished to find her so very lady-like! But she is really quite the gentlewoman.' Mrs Elton is an unjustified snob, ridiculed by Austen as foolish, and so we can assume that a certain class of people would have sneered unjustly at the profession. Yet despite Austen's apparent defence of their merits, there is a sense of panic amongst Highbury when Jane Fairfax commits herself to life as a governess. One is pleased to learn of her engagement to Frank Churchill, if only because it means she will not have to take her post.

But what other option did women have to provide for themselves? Austen's novels frown upon husband hunters like Isabella Thorpe, yet for most women securing themselves a husband was their only hope for a comfortable life. Though they may have been growing increasingly independent in their minds, women lacked the necessary income for their lives to follow suit. In *Pride and Prejudice* Charlotte Lucas accepts a proposal from Mr Collins, a man she never can or will love, because she is conscious of the burden she places on her family's income and the improbability of another proposal so late in life. With her marriage 'the [Lucas] boys were relieved from their apprehension of Charlotte's dying an old maid' as they will escape the cost of a spinster sister weighing on their incomes. Single women were dependent on their fathers and later their brothers – if they were generous enough to assist them, of course. The Dashwood girls' situation in *Sense and Sensibility* arises from their brother's refusal to reduce his son's inheritance to support his sisters:

> 'Consider,' she added, 'that when the money is once parted with, it never can return. Your sisters will marry, and it will be gone for ever. If, indeed, it could ever be restored to our little boy ...'
>
> 'Why, to be sure,' said her husband, very gravely, 'that would make a great difference. The time may come when Harry will regret that so large a sum was parted with. If he should have a numerous family, for instance, it would be a very convenient addition.'

In truth, a girl's only hope of ensuring herself a good home and a steady income was through marriage. It is perhaps a sad reality, and one that Jane's aunt Philadelphia Austen was keenly aware of. Like Jane Fairfax, Philadelphia was an orphan with little fortune and few connections who had been apprenticed to a milliner at 15 years old, a profession that lacked the respectability of a governess and not one that would have likely secured her a respectable husband. With the courage and initiative that characterised the Austen family, Philadelphia abandoned England and sailed for India in search of a husband. Though the journey would have been dangerous for a young woman travelling alone, it was not unheard of or in fact uncommon. India and colonies like it were rife with lonely English gentlemen who were more than happy to marry a poor girl with a pretty smile. Though Philadelphia's marriage to Tysoe Saul Hancock was less than spectacular, it saved her from a life as a milliner and provided her with her beloved daughter, Eliza.

By Heaven! a woman should never be trusted with money.

The Watsons

A young woman, pretty, lively, with a harp as elegant as herself, and both placed near a window, cut down to the ground, and opening on a little lawn, surrounded by shrubs in the rich foliage of summer, was enough to catch any man's heart. The season, the scene, the air, were all favourable to tenderness and sentiment.

Mansfield Park

Emma Woodhouse, handsome, clever and rich, with a comfortable home and happy disposition, seemed to unite some of the best blessings of existence; and had lived nearly twenty-one years in the world with very little to distress or vex her.

Emma

No one who had ever seen Catherine Morland in her infancy would have supposed her born to be an heroine. Her situation in life, the character of her father and mother, her own person and disposition, were all equally against her.

Northanger Abbey

It sometimes happens that a woman is handsomer at twenty-nine than she was ten years before; and, generally speaking, if there has been neither ill health nor anxiety, it is a time of life at which scarcely any charm is lost.

Persuasion

An engaged woman is always more agreeable than a disengaged. She is satisfied with herself. Her cares are over, and she feels that she may exert all her powers of pleasing without suspicion. All is safe with a lady engaged; no harm can be done.

Mansfield Park

Miss Morland, no one can think more highly of the understanding of women than I do. In my opinion, nature has given them so much that they never find it necessary to use more than half.

Northanger Abbey

There are two Traits in her character which are pleasing; namely, she admires Camilla, and drinks no cream in her Tea.

Letter to Cassandra Austen, 15 January 1796

I am pleased that you have learnt to love a hyacinth. The mere habit of learning to love is the thing; and a teachableness of disposition in a young lady is a great blessing.

Northanger Abbey

Harriet certainly was not clever, but she had a sweet docile, grateful disposition, was totally free from conceit, and only desiring to be guided by anyone she looked up to.

Emma

The Miss Dashwoods were young, pretty, and unaffected. It was enough to secure his good opinion, for to be unaffected was all that a pretty girl could want to make her mind as captivating as her person.

Sense and Sensibility

When a young lady is to be a heroine, the perverseness of forty surrounding families cannot prevent her. Something must and will happen to throw a hero in her way.

Northanger Abbey

The Miss Bertrams were now fully established among the belles of the neighbourhood; and as they joined to beauty and brilliant acquirements a manner naturally easy, and carefully formed to general civility and obligingness, they possessed its favour as well as its admiration. Their vanity was in such good order that they seemed to be quite free from it, and gave themselves no airs; while the praises attending such behaviour, secured and brought round by their aunt, served to strengthen them in believing they had no faults.

Mansfield Park

From all that I can collect by your manner of talking, you must be two of the silliest girls in the country. I have suspected it some time, but I am now convinced.

Pride and Prejudice

Ben and Anna walked here last Sunday to hear Uncle Henry, & she looked so pretty, it was quite a pleasure to see her, so young & so blooming & so innocent, as if she had never a wicked Thought in her Life – which yet one has some reason to suppose she must have had, if we believe the Doctrine of Original Sin, or if we remember the events of her girlish days.

Letter to Fanny Knight, 20 February 1817

To look almost pretty is an acquisition of higher delight to a girl who has been looking plain for the first fifteen years of her life than a beauty from her cradle can ever receive.

Northanger Abbey

When a woman has five grown-up daughters, she ought to give over thinking of her own beauty.

Pride and Prejudice

She is not tidy enough in her appearance; she has no dressing-gown to sit up in; her curtains are all too thin, and things are not in that comfort and style about her which are necessary to make such a situation an enviable one.

Letter to Cassandra Austen, 1 December 1798

She cuts her hair too short over her forehead, & does not wear her cap far enough upon her head – in spite of these many disadvantages however, I can still admire her beauty.

Letter to Cassandra Austen, 21 January 1801

A woman, especially if she has the misfortune of knowing anything, should conceal it as well as she can.

Northanger Abbey

I shall not be a poor old maid; and it is poverty only which makes celibacy contemptible to a generous public! A single woman, with a very narrow income, must be a ridiculous, disagreeable old maid!

Emma

She was looking remarkably well; her very regular, very pretty features, having the bloom and freshness of youth restored by the fine wind which had been blowing on her complexion, and by the animations of eye which it had also produced. It was evident that the gentleman (completely a gentleman in manner) admired her exceedingly. Captain Wentworth looked round at her instantly in a way which shewed his noticing of it.

Persuasion

A woman of seven-and-twenty ... can never hope to feel or inspire affection again; and if her home be uncomfortable, or her fortune small, I can suppose that she might bring herself to submit to the offices of a nurse, for the sake of the provision and security of a wife.

Sense and Sensibility

Charles Powett has been very ill, but is getting well again; – his wife is discovered to be everything that the Neighbourhood could wish her, silly and cross as well as extravagant.

Letter to Cassandra Austen, 26 December 1798

They all paint tables, cover screens, and net purses. I scarcely know anyone who cannot do all this, and I am sure I never heard a young lady spoken of for the first time, without being informed that she was very accomplished.

Pride and Prejudice

I am amused by the present style of female dress; – the coloured petticoats with braces over the white Spencers & enormous Bonnets upon the full stretch, are quite entertaining. It seems to me a more marked *change* than one has lately seen.

Letter to Martha Lloyd, 2 September 1814

I have made myself caps to wear of evenings since I came home, and they save me a world of torment as to hairdressing, which at present gives me no trouble beyond washing and brushing, for my long hair is always plaited up out of sight, and my short hair curls well enough to want no papering.

Letter to Cassandra Austen, 1 December 1798

A single woman, of good fortune, is always respectable, and may be as sensible and pleasant as anybody else.

Emma

Single Women have a dreadful propensity for being poor – which is one very strong argument in favour of Matrimony.

Letter to Fanny Knight, 13 March 1817

A woman can never be too fine while she is all in white.

Mansfield Park

A lady, without a family, was the very best preserver of furniture in the world.

Persuasion

I wish I could help you in your Needlework, I have two hands & a new thimble that lead a very easy life.

Letter to Cassandra Austen, 27 December 1808

If adventures will not befall a young lady in her own village, she must seek them abroad.

Northanger Abbey

Henrietta and Louisa, young ladies of nineteen and twenty, who had brought from school at Exeter all the usual stock of accomplishments, and were now like thousands of other young ladies, living to be fashionable, happy, and merry. Their dress had every advantage, their faces were rather pretty, their spirits extremely good, their manner unembarrassed and pleasant; they were of consequence at home, and favourites abroad.

Persuasion

A girl of fifteen! the very age of all others to need most attention and care, and put the cheerfullest spirits to the test!

Mansfield Park

That will do extremely well, child. You have delighted us long enough. Let the other young ladies have time to exhibit.

Pride and Prejudice

I am glad to hear such a good account of Harriot Bridges; she goes on now as young Ladies of 17 ought to do; admired & admiring; in a much more rational way than her three elder Sisters, who had so little of that kind of Youth.

Letter to Cassandra Austen, 9 January 1799

If you cannot bear an uncle's admiration, what is to become of you? You must really begin to harden yourself to the idea of being worth looking at. You must try not to mind growing up into a pretty woman.

Mansfield Park

She is quite the Anna with variations – but she cannot have reached her last, for that is always the most flourishing & shewey – she is at about her 3rd or 4th which are generally simple and pretty.

Letter to Cassandra Austen, 25 April 1811

A lady's imagination is very rapid; it jumps from admiration to love, from love to matrimony, in a moment.

Pride and Prejudice

Young ladies should take care of themselves. Young ladies are delicate plants. They should take care of their health and their complexion.

Emma

Lady Middleton was equally pleased with Mrs Dashwood. There was a kind of cold-hearted selfishness on both sides, which mutually attracted them; and they sympathised with each other in an insipid propriety of demeanour, and a general want of understanding.

Sense and Sensibility

I can perfectly comprehend Mrs Cage's distress & perplexity. – She has all those kind of foolish & incomprehensible feelings which would make her fancy herself uncomfortable in such a party. – I love her in spite of all her Nonsense.

Letter to Cassandra Austen, 9 January 1799

A young lady who faints, must be recovered; questions must be answered, and surprises be explained. Such events are very interesting, but the suspense of them cannot last long.

Emma

Beware of fainting-fits ... Though at the time they may be refreshing and agreeable, yet believe me they will in the end, if too often repeated and at improper seasons, prove destructive to your Constitution ... My fate will teach you this ... I die a Martyr to my grief for the loss of Augustus ... One fatal swoon has cost me my Life ... Beware of swoons, Dear Laura ... A frenzy fit is not one quarter so pernicious; it is an exercise to the Body and if not too violent, is, I dare say, conducive to Health in its consequences – Run mad as often as you chuse; but do not faint.

Love and Freinship [sic]

Young women should always be properly guarded and attended, according to their situation in life.

Pride and Prejudice

Had she been older or vainer, such attacks might have done little; but, where youth and diffidence are united, it requires uncommon steadiness of reason to resist the attraction of being called the most charming girl in the world.

Northanger Abbey

I should say she was a good-tempered girl, not likely to be very, very determined against any young man who told her he loved her.

Emma

Oh! Dear Fanny, Your mistake has been one that thousands of women fall into. He was the *first* young Man who attached himself to you. That was the charm, & most powerful it is.

Letter to Fanny Knight, 18 November 1814

My mind was very agreeably engaged. I have been meditating on the very great pleasure which a pair of fine eyes in the face of a pretty woman can bestow.

Pride and Prejudice

Without thinking highly of either of men or matrimony, marriage had always been her object; it was the only provision for well-educated young women of small fortune, and however uncertain of giving happiness, must be their pleasantest preservative from want.

Pride and Prejudice

I am sorry I have affronted you on the subject of Mr Moore, but I do not mean ever to like him; & as to pitying a young woman merely because she cannot live in two places at the same time, & at once enjoy the comforts of being married and single, I shall attempt it.

Letter to Cassandra Austen, 8 February 1807

Speak your opinion, for ladies can best tell the taste of ladies in regard to places as well as men.

Northanger Abbey

Give a girl an education, and introduce her properly into the world, and ten to one but she has the means of settling well, without farther expense to anybody.

Mansfield Park

She is tolerable, but not handsome enough to tempt *me*; I am in no humour at present to give consequence to young ladies who are slighted by other men.

Pride and Prejudice

You have proved yourself upright and disinterested, prove yourself grateful and tender-hearted; and then you will be the perfect model of a woman which I have always believed you born for.

Mansfield Park

Her days of insignificance and evil were over. – She would soon be well, and happy, and prosperous.

Emma

Her mind, disposition, opinion, and habits wanted no half-concealment, no self-deception on the present, no reliance on future improvement. Even in the midst of his late infatuation, he had acknowledged Fanny's mental superiority.

Mansfield Park

Marianne was silent; it was impossible for her to say what she did not feel, however trivial the occasion.

Sense and Sensibility

Do not consider me now an elegant female, intending to plague you, but as a rational creature, speaking the truth from her heart.

Pride and Prejudice

We have heard nothing fresh from Anna. I trust she is very comfortable in her new home. Her Letters have been very sensible & satisfactory with no *parade* of happiness, which I liked them the better for. – I have often known young married Women write in a way I did not like, in that respect.

Letter to Fanny Knight, 18 November 1814

What did she say? Just what she ought, of course. A lady always does. She said enough to shew there need to be despair – and to invite him to say more himself.

Emma

Catherine did not know her own advantages – did not know that a good-looking girl, with an affectionate heart and a very ignorant mind, cannot fail of attracting a clever young man, unless circumstances are particularly untoward.

Northanger Abbey

It is sometimes a disadvantage to be so very guarded. If a woman conceals her affection with the same skill from the object of it, she may lose the opportunity of fixing him.

Pride and Prejudice

Woman is fine for her own satisfaction alone. No man will admire her the more, no woman will like her the better for it. Neatness and fashion are enough for the former, and a something of shabbiness or impropriety will be most endearing to the latter.

Northanger Abbey

I will not allow it to be more man's nature than woman's to be inconstant and forget those they do love, or have loved. I believe the reverse. I believe in a true analogy between our bodily frames and our mental; and that as our bodies are the strongest, so are our feelings; capable of bearing most rough usage, and riding out the heaviest weather.

Persuasion

There was no getting at her real opinion. Wrapt up in a cloak of politeness, she seemed determined to hazard nothing. She was disgustingly, was suspiciously reserved.

Emma

Yes. We certainly do not forget you so soon as you forget us. It is, perhaps, our fate rather than our merit. We cannot help ourselves. We live at home, quiet, confined, and our feelings prey upon us.

Persuasion

To be so bent on marriage – to pursue a man merely for the sake of situation – is a sort of thing that shocks me; I cannot understand it. Poverty is a great evil, but to a woman of education and feeling it ought not, it cannot be the greatest. – I would rather be a teacher at a school (and I can think of nothing worse) than marry a man I did not like.

The Watsons

I suppose all the world is sitting in Judgement upon the Princess of Wales's Letter. Poor Woman, I shall support her as long as I can, because she *is* a Woman, & because I hate her Husband – but I can hardly forgive her for calling herself 'attached & affectionate' to a Man whom she must detest.

Letter to Martha Lloyd, 16 February 1813

· 3 ·

FAMILY

IN THE INTIMATE, DOMESTIC scope of Jane Austen's work, familial life and relationships play an important and irrefutable role; one might even say that the fact that family is a significant concern in any Austen novel is 'a truth universally acknowledged'. Austen opens up houses such as Hartfield and Longbourn as if they were dolls' houses, and allows her readers to peer inside as she brings the inhabiting families to life. Austen's families are unfailingly entertaining; tinged with absurdity, they function on outdated notions and misunderstood social conventions. Mothers are frequently absent or ineffective: Mrs Woodhouse and Lady Elliot are both deceased before either of their respective daughters; Fanny Price has little contact with her mother and Catherine Morland's adventures all occur away from home. Mrs Dashwood, meanwhile, is too caring, indulging Marianne's romantic sensibilities and relying on Elinor for sense instead of providing it herself. As for Jane and Elizabeth Bennet, the very chance at matrimony so desired by Mrs Bennet is nearly ruined by her behaviour and her failure to manage that of the younger girls. Fathers receive little better treatment from Austen's pen: other than his respectability Mr Morland gets little mention, whilst the Dashwood girls have no father. Mr Price is an alcoholic with no interest in his daughters and Sir Walter Elliot, pompous and preening, is ridiculed by Austen. Mr Woodhouse and Mr Bennet may have considerably more affection for their daughters but their social detachment and disinterested lifestyles allows the girls' flaws and faults to go unchecked.

Austen creates families that are amusing and entertaining, with just enough ridiculousness to remain relatable and realistic. But for Austen herself, just how realistic were such families? Jane Austen was one of eight children, the younger daughter of a middle-class country clergyman. The family's status and situation would have been much the same as the Morlands and the Bennets: large, respectable families with comfortable but unimpressive incomes. George Austen certainly worked hard to provide for his family, supplementing his clergyman's income by running a small boarding school for the sons of gentlemen within the Rectory at Steventon. Born in 1731, George Austen and his two sisters, Leonora and Philadelphia, were left orphaned at an early age. Whilst his sisters were left in the care of their uncle, Stephen Austen, George was to have another uncle as his patron: Francis Austen of Sevenoaks, Kent. Francis, who had earned both fortune and reputation as a lawyer, funded his nephew's education, first at the Tonbridge School and at St John's College, Oxford. It seems that George Austen proved himself to be a capable and interested scholar and would serve

Edward Austen, Jane's wealthy elder brother.

at Tonbridge as second master before returning to Oxford to take his orders. As well as being known as a great reader and a particular champion of novels, George's good looks had earned him a nickname: 'the handsome proctor'. His granddaughter, James' daughter Anna Austen, later remembered him worthy of such a reputation:

> As a young man I have always understood that he was considered extremely handsome, and it was a beauty which stood by him all his life. At the time when I have the most perfect recollection of him he must have been hard upon seventy, but his hair in its milk-whiteness might have belonged to a much older man. It was very beautiful, with short curls about the ears. His eyes were not large, but of a peculiar and bright hazel. My aunt Jane's were something like them, but none of the children had precisely the same excepting my uncle Henry.

Handsome and intelligent, George Austen seems to have maintained a balanced family life too; he was undoubtedly in love with his wife and affectionate with his children, but he was also rational and hard working. He educated his daughters as well as his sons, lived mostly within his means and helped the boys into suitable careers. His letter to his son Francis on his first sea voyage with the navy aged just 14 reveals much of George's personality as a father; it advises his son in proper conduct and manners and sensible money management, but also assures his young son of his family's love for him and is signed:

I have nothing more to add but my blessing and best prayers for your health and prosperity, and to beg you would never forget you have not upon earth a more disinterested and warm friend than, your truly affectionate father, George Austen.

Such a father certainly could hardly be the inspiration for the likes of Sir Walter Elliot! Indeed, Jane Austen greatly admired her father and received much of her literary passions from him. Whilst there is some of Mr Austen's character in Mr Bennet, there is none of his engaged nature: Jane's father greatly enjoyed society and saw much of his friends and family, both as a host and as visitor.

However, if there is little trace of Jane's own father in those of her heroines, there is perhaps even less of her mother in the likes of Mrs Bennet or even Mrs Dashwood. Anna Austen remembered her grandmother, born Cassandra Leigh in 1739, as being:

A little, slight woman, with fine, well-cut features, large grey eyes, and good eyebrows, but without any brightness of complexion. She was amusingly particular about people's noses, having a very aristocratic one herself, which she had the pleasure of transmitting to a good many of her children. She was a quick-witted woman with plenty of sparkle and spirit in her talk, who could write an excellent letter, either in prose or verse, making no pretence to poetry but being simply playful common sense in rhyme.

Cassandra's nose was not the only thing aristocratic about her. The Leigh family, descended from a Lord Mayor of London, were proud of their lineage and history. Cassandra's own grandmother, Mary Brydges, was sister to the Duke of Chandos and though her own father was a clergyman, her Leigh cousins were wealthy landowners. She was also connected academically: her uncle Theophilus Leigh was master of Balliol College, Oxford, from 1726 until his death in 1785. It's possible that George and Cassandra might have had their first meeting at Oxford, but it was in Bath that the couple courted and later married. George, with handsome looks and a bright mind, and Cassandra, sharp and sensible, were a well-matched couple and kept a rational, economic household. Mrs Austen would have been as involved in the children's education as her husband and Jane would have greatly benefitted from her mother's striking wit and good sense. A scholarly, affectionate father with a passion for novels and a quick, clever mother must have been the perfect combination for nurturing a talent such as Jane's.

Jane Austen certainly had no short supply of male inspiration growing up surrounded by her brothers, whilst her sister Cassandra would be everything from friend, to confidante and editor. Jane's letters reveal a close-knit family,

teasing and affectionate as well as helpful and supportive.
When their father's death left their mother and sisters with
a greatly reduced income, the Austen brothers were quick to
pledge part of their own incomes for their comfort. Jane's
admiration and fondness for her brothers can be found not
only in her letters, but in some of her heroes. *Northanger
Abbey*'s Henry Tilney is a caring, lively brother – particularly
when contrasted by his 'rival', the odious John Thorpe – and
part of Elizabeth Bennet's change of opinion of Mr Darcy
comes from observing his tenderness towards his sister.

The eldest of the Austen children, James (born 1765),
shared his youngest sister's literary aspirations. As well as
an interest in poetry, James was the organiser of many of
Steventon's amateur dramatics, performed by the children
along with neighbours and cousins for entertainment at
holidays or for visiting relatives. These performances – which
included Elizabeth Inchbald's *Lovers Vows*, the same play chosen
by the Bertrams for their ill-fated theatricals in *Mansfield Park*
– would often feature introductions or epilogues penned by
James. After being educated at home with his brothers and
his father's pupils, James left for Oxford at just 14 years
old, with a 'Founders Kin' scholarship for St John's College
thanks to a distant relation on his mother's side. Like his
father, James seems to have been quite the scholar and suc-
ceeded in his studies. After a brief tour of Europe James
returned to Oxford to take his orders and was ordained in
1787. However, James had not forgotten his literary tastes
and, along with his younger brother Henry, who was now
also at Oxford, began to publish a weekly magazine called

The Loiterer. The publication was inspired by the *Rambler* and the *Idler*, which belonged to the great Dr Johnson, and each issue would feature an anonymous essay or story. *The Loiterer* only ran for a little more than a year, but it's likely that its mild success had an impact on the young Jane Austen.

"*Dear, dear, Norland! when shall I cease to regret you*"

Marianne bids goodbye to Norland Park. (*Sense and Sensibility*, Chris Hammond)

James' first wife was an Anne Matthew: wealthy, well connected and, at 32, rather past her prime by Georgian standards. In 1793 the couple welcomed their first and only child, a little girl christened Jane Anna Elizabeth and known to her family just as Anna. Two years later, Anne suddenly and unexpectedly passed away leaving James a widower and little Anna motherless. As was natural for men in James' situation, he began to look for a new wife and found one in the Austen's former neighbour, Mary Lloyd. Though Mary, along with her sister Martha, had been close friends with the Austen girls, it appears that Jane found her less favourable as a sister-in-law. Jane had once admired her brother as a writer and, in an early letter, as great company at a ball, but in a letter to Cassandra dated 8 February 1807, she lamented that:

> I am sorry & angry that his Visits should not give one more pleasure; – the company of so good & so clever a Man ought to be gratifying in itself but his Chat seems all forced, his Opinions on many points too much copied from his Wife.

His marriage to Mary would produce two more children, a son, James Edward, and a daughter, Caroline. James Edward would later inherit his maternal Great Uncle James Leigh Perrot's fortune and add his grandmother's maiden name to his grandfather's. As James Edward Austen Leigh he would have a house and a fair fortune, but for the Austen family perhaps his greatest importance was as Jane's first biographer. With help from his sisters and cousins, it was James Edward, having once hoped to be a writer like his Aunt Jane, who kept Austen's memory alive and sparked the revival in her popularity.

The Austens' second child was born in 1766, another boy, to be named George after his father. However, whilst his brothers grew sturdy and strong, letters from Mr and Mrs Austen speak their fears for their second son. George's development was much slower than James' and his parents mention a number of fits in their letters. It's still unclear what ailed poor George Austen, though cases for epilepsy and cerebral palsy have been made. Many critics suspect that George may have been deaf, as Jane mentions speaking to a deaf gentleman using her fingers in a letter to Cassandra in 1808. What we do know is that Georgian society's ideas were less than kind towards disabilities and handicaps and so disabled children were often hidden from the public eye, their existence denied. Though the 2007 film *Becoming Jane* depicts an adult George living at Steventon with his family, the majority of his life was spent in the care of a family called Culham in the village of Monk Sherborne, near Basingstoke. Considering their busy lives and ever-growing family, and the concern for George in their letters, it seems his removal was more for the sake of his care and comfort than a matter of public pride or appearance. Mrs Austen's younger brother Thomas had been in the Culham family's care for a number of years, so the Austens must have been certain of their son being well looked after there. Though George is absent from Jane's letters, and in fact from James Edward's *Memoir*, his family could not have forgotten him – his care continued to be paid for, funded by his younger brother Edward after the death of their parents.

Of all the Austen siblings, it would have been Edward who was most able to assist his brother. The living of Steventon was part of the estate of Thomas Knight, a distant cousin of Mr Austen's, along with another Hampshire village, Chawton and Godmersham in Kent. In 1799 the newly married Mr Knight took his bride on a tour of his property, including a visit to the Austens at Steventon Rectory. Edward Austen would have been 12 years old and, though not as intellectual as James, showed a good heart and an honest, steady character. Mrs Catherine Knight was pleased with him immediately, so much so that he was invited to join them for the rest of their honeymoon tour – an odd request perhaps for newly-weds but undoubtedly one that would entirely alter Edward's fortune. For the next few years Edward was invited to Godmersham Park to spend holidays, and as they continued to be childless they began to think of Edward as their own. The Knights' estate was large and in need of an heir, but their marriage failed to produce one. In the church that sits behind Godmersham Park is a marble plaque commemorating Thomas Knight and above its inscription is a broken pillar: the Knight line was broken. Instead, the now 16-year-old Edward Austen was officially adopted, to take the name of Knight when he inherited the estates.

Under the care of his adoptive parents, Edward Austen began to grow into a gentleman. Instead of university he was sent to take the Grand Tour, spending two years travelling Europe and settling at Godmersham with the Knights on his return. In 1791 he married Elizabeth Bridges, one of the elegant daughters of another respectable Kent family, with whom he would have eleven children. A few years after his marriage saw the death of Thomas Knight, and his widow decided to vacate Godmersham for Edward and his quickly growing family. When Edward, with his good heart and honest nature, wrote to insist that she could not give up her home for them, Mrs Knight responded:

From the time that my partiality for you induced Mr. Knight to treat you as our adopted child I have felt for you the tenderness of a mother, and never have you appeared more deserving of affection than at this time; to reward your merit, therefore, and to place you in a situation where your many excellent qualities will be called forth and rendered useful to the neighbourhood, is the fondest wish of my heart. Many circumstances attached to large landed possessions, highly gratifying to a man, are entirely lost on me at present; but when I see you in the enjoyment of them, I shall, if possible, feel my gratitude to my beloved husband redoubled, for having placed in my hands the power of bestowing happiness on one so very dear to me.

Edward was persuaded to allow his adoptive mother to take a house in Canterbury and moved his wife and children into the great house at Godmersham. Though Jane spent less time in Kent than Cassandra, who often came to help Elizabeth manage the house during her pregnancies, Edward's life as a landed gentleman and his home had a great impact on her. Without Edward's adoption, Jane may never have experienced life in the upper classes well enough to craft them so impressively in her novels. Elegant and stately, with an awe-inspiring view, Godmersham Park must have helped Austen to create houses such as Pemberley and Mansfield Park, whilst her brother's life as a gentleman and landlord allowed her to understand the lifestyles and pressures of their masters. As for Edward himself, his income would have been greater even than Mr Darcy's impressive £10,000 a year, allowing him to provide comfortably for his mother and sisters as well as his own brood of eleven, supplementing their income after his father's death and renovating Chawton Cottage for them in 1809. Certainly this example of true gentlemanly behaviour must have inspired Austen's pen; *Emma*'s Mr Knightley seems to possess many of her rich brother's traits. Perhaps Edward Knight, generous, steady and unfailingly good, even lent his adopted name to one of Jane's heroes?

After three sons, 1773 would bring the Austens their first daughter. She would be Cassandra, after her mother and countless other Leigh relatives, and said to resemble her brother Edward – whilst Jane resembled Henry and Mr Austen. The close bond between the Austen sisters began in childhood and was so strong that their mother once remarked that 'If Cassandra were going to have her head cut off, Jane would insist on sharing her fate'.

Indeed, when Cassandra was to be sent to school in Oxford with their cousin, Jane Cooper, Jane Austen's refusal to be left behind by her sister led to her attending with them despite, at just 7, being too young to be from home. However, as the Austen sisters grew older, familial and social obligation meant that separation was unavoidable and so they became frequent correspondents. Though their time apart may not have been appreciated by Jane, for her fans and biographers it has become something of a blessing. Though Cassandra burned many of her sister's letters, thought to be those that contained details that were too personal or revealing, and cut sections of others, they have been the key to unlocking Jane Austen. To Cassandra, not just her sister but her most trusted, beloved friend and advisor, Jane expressed her most honest opinions on everything from fashion to food. With so little other biographical record, the letters to Cassandra have been crucial in piecing together the events of Austen's life, as well as allowing us to understand her mind and personality.

Next born at Steventon would be Henry Austen in 1771; charming, handsome, he would often be a favourite in society and certainly with his younger sister. Said to share their father's features, Henry and Jane also shared a talent for wit and a lively spirit. Anna Austen remembered him as such:

My Uncle Henry Thomas Austen was the handsomest of his family, and, in the opinion of his own father, also the most talented. There were others who formed a different estimate, and considered his abilities greater in shew than in reality, but for the most part he was greatly admired. Brilliant in conversation, and like his Father, blessed with a hopefulness of temper, which, in adapting itself to all circumstances, even the most adverse, seemed to create a perpetual sunshine of the mind.

Though Henry followed his eldest brother to Oxford, he lacked James' studious nature and turned away from the life of a clergyman (initially) in favour of position in the militia. With the Napoleonic Wars raging overseas, the army became a good prospect for many young men and Henry Austen seems to have been attracted to its possibilities for greatness and excitement. Tall and striking, Henry must have cut a fine figure in his red coat – much like a certain other officer in *Pride and Prejudice*. Henry, who pursued his elegant French cousin and engaged himself to a Miss Pearson, appears to have had a rather flirtatious nature as well as taste for fine society and its lifestyle. After his military career failed to bring him sufficient riches and glory Henry moved to London to set himself up as banker, which provided an income to keep himself and kept Eliza entertained. It seems likely that some of Henry's less amiable behaviour was used by Jane as the inspiration for the deceptively charming and badly behaved young men in her novels, such as Mr Wickham and Henry Crawford. But though Henry lends his name to one of Jane's 'villains', it is also bestowed upon *Northanger Abbey*'s lively, intelligent hero Henry Tilney. In fact, Henry Austen would be the greatest hero of any of his sister's works, for they would have never have reached publication without his help: his banking business may have paid for his London lifestyle, but it also allowed him to act as his sister's literary agent. It would be Henry who approached the publishers, worked out deals and helped Jane to achieve her anonymous popularity. Despite his early protestations, Henry Austen did eventually turn to a career in the Church when, in the peace after the Battle of Waterloo, Henry's business failed and he was bankrupted.

In 1809, Jane Austen wrote to her fifth brother Francis in the form of a poem to congratulate him on the birth of his first son, expressing a desire to see the young boy grow up to be much like his father:

Endow'd with Art's and Nature's Good,
Thy Name possessing with thy Blood,
In him, in all his ways, may we
Another Francis William see! –
Thy infant days may he inherit,
Thy warmth, nay insolence of spirit; –
We would not with one foult dispense
To weaken the resemblance.
May he revive thy Nursery sin,
Peeping as daringly within,

His curley Locks but just descried,
With 'Bet, my be not come to bide.'

The poem, apart from showing Austen's affection as a sister and an aunt, gives an insight into the character of the Austens' sixth child, a boy who grew up to claim the title of Admiral Sir Francis Austen. Francis, nicknamed Frank or sometimes, Fly seems to have been adventurous even from early childhood. Apart from being the leader amongst the youngest Austens, Francis was practical and determined – he somehow managed to buy himself a pony aged just 7 and quickly took to hunting in a red riding habit his mother had fashioned for him from her wedding clothes. Francis joined the Royal Naval Academy in Portsmouth at 12 years old, where he proved himself to be a more than capable pupil and sailed for the East Indies aged 14. Within the year he was promoted to midshipman and would continue to enjoy an exemplary career as naval officer. Though his ascent through the ranks was perhaps assisted by the Austen family's naval connections, Francis was undoubtedly an outstanding sailor; he was even referred to by Lord Nelson as 'an excellent young man'. In 1795 his ship, the *Lark*, was also part of the squadron that accompanied Princess Caroline of Brunswick to England for her marriage to the Prince of Wales. Frank married Mary Gibson in 1806 and settled in Southampton, where they invited Jane, Cassandra and Mrs Austen to stay, which for Jane was a welcome chance to escape from Bath. Like his elder brother Edward, Francis' marriage to Mary produced eleven children and, like Elizabeth, Mary's health never recovered after the birth of their last child. Francis would later marry Martha Lloyd, his sisters' lifelong friend and companion at Chawton.

Though Jane didn't live to see her brother's promotion to admiral, she closely followed his career and her letters to him betray a great deal of pride and love for him. The navy would be the making of Francis Austen: it bought him fortune, respectability and title. Jane's defence of Captain Wentworth in *Persuasion* against the shallow snobbery of Sir Walter Elliot reveals the struggle of young men like Francis Austen against the prejudices of an older generation, as well as her respect for his profession. Excepting Jane, the Austens were a remarkably well-lived family; Frank lived to the age of 91, outliving his parents and siblings.

If Francis was Jane's Captain Wentworth, than Charles Austen must have been her William Price. Born in 1779, Charles was the last of the Austens children and a particular favourite with Jane, perhaps as he was the only sibling younger than she. He was to be her and Cassandra's 'own particular little brother' and was as tender to his sisters as they were to him. Like *Mansfield Park*'s William Price, Charles used his share of the money from a successful privateer to purchase topaz crosses for his beloved sisters, which they happily reproached him for. Poor Charles, though a good sailor, did not enjoy the same success as his elder brother. Like Francis, he entered the naval academy at 12 years old and by 18 had been made lieutenant and, again like William Price, was anxious to be able to prove himself worthy of promotion. In 1804 he was posted to the North America Station, where he would remain for the next seven years. His loneliness was soon cured with an engagement to 16-year-old Fanny Palmer, the pretty daughter of an English lawyer in Bermuda. The couple were married in 1807, but it would be another four years and the birth of two daughters before Charles returned to his family. In 1810 his career began to improve, when he was given command of the *Swiftsure*, the flagship of Admiral Sir John Borlase Warren. However, Fanny's death in 1814 brought tragedy to his family and in 1816 Charles' ship was wrecked whilst pursuing pirates. He wasn't given another command for ten years and his finances struggled greatly, as did Charles; not only was his income reduced, his daughter Harriet became seriously ill. He went on to marry Fanny's sister Harriet in 1820, not uncommon for a widower at this time, and would eventually be made rear admiral in 1846. Both he and Francis would actively serve in the navy into old age; Charles died of cholera whilst at sea, aged 71.

Can it be any wonder that such a vibrant, talented family created a timeless talent like Jane Austen's? Though her heroines may not be blessed with the same clever and affectionate siblings as she was, their influence on her opinions and her abilities is evident. Jane Bennet and Elinor Dashwood are blessed with Cassandra Austen's sense and tenderness as elder sister, whilst Austen's handsome heroes are often rather flattering compliments to her brothers and their professions. For a woman like Austen, who invested much pride in her siblings and valued her position as an aunt, the importance of family must have been an undeniable truth.

It is very unfair to judge of any body's conduct, without an intimate knowledge of their situation. Nobody, who has not been in the interior of a family, can say what the difficulties of any individual of that family may be.

Emma

On his two younger sisters he then bestowed an equal portion of his fraternal tenderness, for he asked each of them how they both did, and observed that they both looked very ugly.

Northanger Abbey

In everything but disposition they were admirably taught. Sir Thomas did not know what was wanting, because, though a truly anxious father, he was not outwardly affectionate, and the reserve of his manner repressed all the flow of their spirits before him.

Mansfield Park

Between Barton and Delaford, there was that constant communication which strong family affection would naturally dictate; and among the merits and the happiness of Elinor and Marianne, let it not be ranked as the least considerable, that though sisters, and living almost within sight of each other, they could live without disagreement between themselves, or producing coolness between their husbands.

Sense and Sensibility

They never once thought of her heart, which, for the parents of a young lady of seventeen, just returned from her first excursion from home, was odd enough!

Northanger Abbey

But Tom's extravagance had, previous to that event, been so great as to render a different disposal of the next presentation necessary, and the younger brother must help to pay for the pleasures of the elder.

Mansfield Park

Husbands and wives generally understand when opposition will be vain.

Persuasion

An unhappy alternative is before you, Elizabeth. From this day you must be a stranger to one of your parents. Your mother will never see you again if you do not marry Mr. Collins, and I will never see you again if you do.

Pride and Prejudice

Lady Bertram did not go into public with her daughters. She was too indolent even to accept a mother's gratification in witnessing their success and enjoyment at the expense of any personal trouble.

Mansfield Park

If my children are silly, I must hope to be always sensible of it.

Pride and Prejudice

Now that you are become an Aunt, you are a person of some consequence & must excite a great Interest whatever You do. I have always maintained the importance of Aunts as much as possible.

Letter to Caroline Austen, 30 October 1815

Having never been able to glory in beauty of her own, she thoroughly enjoyed the power in being proud of her sisters.

Mansfield Park

I do not mean to say that a woman may not be settled too near her family. The far and the near must be relative, and depend on many varying expenses of travelling. Where there is fortune to make the expenses of travelling unimportant, distance becomes no evil.

Pride and Prejudice

What strange creatures brothers are! You would not write to each other but upon the most urgent necessity in the world; and when obliged to take up the pen to say that such a horse is ill, or such a relation dead, it is done in the fewest possible words. You have but one style among you. I know it perfectly. Henry, who is in every other respect exactly what a brother should be, who loves me, consults me, confides in me, and will talk to me by the hour together, has never yet turned the page in a letter; and very often it is nothing more than – 'Dear Mary, I am just arrived. Bath seems full, and everything as usual. Yours sincerely.' That is the true manly style; that is a complete brother's letter.

Mansfield Park

Henry heard [*Pride and Prejudice*] warmly praised in Scotland, by Lady Robert Kerr & another Lady; – & what does he do in the warmth of his Brotherly vanity & Love; but immediately tell them who wrote it! – A Thing once set going in that way – one knows how it spreads!

Letter to Francis Austen, 25 September 1813

A well-disposed young woman, who did not marry for love, was in general but the more attached to her own family.

Mansfield Park

After abusing you so abominably to your face, I could have no scruple in abusing you to all your relations.

Pride and Prejudice

But it is very foolish to ask questions about any young ladies – about any three sisters just grown up; for one knows, without being told, exactly what they are – all very accomplished and pleasing, and one very pretty. There is a beauty in every family. – It is a regular thing.

Mansfield Park

I think it would be very hard upon younger sisters, that they should not have their share of society and amusement, because the elder may not have the means or inclination to marry early.

Pride and Prejudice

I am greatly pleased with your account of Fanny; I found her in the summer just what you describe, almost another Sister; & could not have supposed that a niece would ever have been so much to me.

Letter to Cassandra Austen, 7 October 1808

Oh! what a loss it will be, when you are married. You are too agreeable in your single state, too agreeable as a Niece. I shall hate you when your delicious play of Mind is all settled down in to conjugal & maternal affections.

Letter to Fanny Knight, 20 February 1817

I believe there is scarcely a young lady in the United Kingdoms who would not rather put up with the misfortune of being sought by a clever agreeable man, than have him driven away by the vulgarity of her nearest relations.

Mansfield Park

A younger son, you know, must be inured to self-denial and dependence.

Pride and Prejudice

Oh! your father of course may spare you, if your mother can. Daughters are never of so much consequence to a father.

Pride and Prejudice

Frank and Mary are cannot at all approve of your not being home in time to help them in their finishing purchases … they shall be spiteful as possible and chuse everything in the stile most likely to vex you, Knives that will not cut, glasses that will not hold, a sofa without a seat, & a Bookcase without shelves.

Letter to Cassandra Austen, 8 February 1807

Even the smooth surface of family-union seems worth preserving, though there may be nothing durable beneath.

Persuasion

Her power was sinking; everything *must* sink under such a proof of family weakness, such an assurance at the deepest disgrace.

Pride and Prejudice

How to do justice the kindness of all my family during this illness, is quite beyond me! – Every dear Brother so affectionate & so anxious! – And my sister! – Words must fail me in any attempt to describe what a Nurse she has been to me.

Letter to Anne Sharp, 22 May 1817

I have melancholy news to relate, & sincerely feel for your feelings under the shock of it. – I wish I could better prepare You for it. – But having said so much, Your mind already forestall the sort of Event which I have to communicate. – Our dear Father has closed his virtuous & happy life, in a death almost as free from suffering as his Children could have wished.

Letter to Francis Austen, 21 January 1805

In short, if I live to be an old Woman I must expect to wish I had died now, blessed by the tenderness of such a Family & before I had survived either them or their affection.

Letter to Anne Sharp, 22 May 1817

YM RAED YSSAC,

I hsiw uoy a yppah wen raey. Ruoy xis snisuoc emac ereh yadretsey, dna dah hcae a eceip of ekac. Siht si elttil Yssac's yadhtrib, dna ehs si eerht sraey dlo. Knarf sah nugeb gninrael Nital. Ew deef eht Nibor yreve gninrom. Yllas netfo seriuqne retfa uoy. Yllas Mahneb sah tog a wen neerg nwog. Teirrah Thgink semoc yreve yad ot daer ot Tnua Ardnassac. Doog eyb, ym raed Yssac.

Tnua Ardnassac sdnes reh tseb evol, dna os ew od lla.

Ruoy etanoitceffa Tnua, ENAJ NETSUA.

Letter to Cassy Esten Austen, Charles Austen's daughter, 8 January 1817

4

SOCIETY & MANNERS

THOUGH HER WORK IS now considered to be definitive of the British Regency, Jane Austen thought very little of the Prince Regent himself. She was disgusted by his behaviour towards his wife, and seems to have generally disapproved of his extravagant lifestyle. Yet *Emma*, the last of Austen's novels to be published in her lifetime, is dedicated to none of than the Prince Regent. The dedication was not sought by Austen; instead it came about after a chance meeting in London. Henry Austen had become unwell during Jane's visit, and his doctor requested a second opinion from a man who was also physician to the Prince Regent. When Jane's identity as the author of *Sense and Sensibility* and *Pride and Prejudice* was discovered, the prince was claimed to be an admirer, supposedly with a set of her novels in each of his houses. Whether or not the claim was true (his daughter Charlotte had read *Sense and Sensibility*) was irrelevant, and Jane received an invitation to have tea at Carlton House with the prince's librarian, James Stanier Clarke, who gave her permission to dedicate her next novel to the prince. Despite her dislike for him, Austen could hardly refuse such a prestigious honour and so *Emma* was dedicated:

To
His Royal Highness the Prince Regent,
This work is,
By His Royal Highness's permission,
Most respectfully
Dedicated
By His Royal Highness's
Dutiful
And obedient
Humble servant,
the Author.

But who was this Prince Regent that Jane Austen so poorly regarded? Prince George Augustus Frederick of Wales was the eldest son of King George III and his wife, Queen Charlotte, and the heir to the British throne. Where his father had been steady and honest, the prince was fine in his tastes and frivolous with his money. His residence in London, Carlton House, would be, to borrow a phrase from Austen, a scene of dissipation and vice. The Prince of Wales' life became one of excess and indulgence, and not without scandal. George enjoyed a number of illicit affairs and, in 1785, an illegal marriage to Maria Fitzherbert, a twice widowed commoner and a Catholic. But such a lifestyle was expensive, and the prince soon found himself deep in debts that his father refused to pay. By 1795 his arrears must have been extortionate, as he

Such very superior dancing is not often seen.

Conversations at Netherfield ball. (*Pride and Prejudice*, Hugh Thomson)

agreed to marry Princess Caroline of Brunswick – his father's condition for clearing his debts. Their marriage was an utter disaster; after the birth of Princess Charlotte in 1796 the prince promptly separated himself from his wife (the pair were never to be on civil terms) and resumed his life of vice and excess without hesitation.

King George III's health had been in decline for some time and in 1810 he suffered a malady that would become known as his 'madness' after the death of his beloved youngest daughter, Princess Amelia. Almost blind from cataracts and distraught over his daughter's death, the British Parliament deemed the king unfit for rule and passed the Regency Act of 1811. On 5 February 1811, the Prince of Wales was elevated to Prince Regent. Though the term is used for a slightly broader period in history, this would be the beginning of British Regency.

George, now Prince Regent, continued to indulge his expensive tastes, particularly architecture and interior design. Carlton House was to be kept fashionable and suitably splendid and Brighton Pavilion was to be renovated as an exotic, Oriental-inspired seaside retreat for the prince. Though they were more than a little extravagant, the Prince Regent's tastes in art and architecture were good and privileged society began to flourish under his care. Lavish feasts attended by the social elite were to be held in rooms of refined elegance; and, of course, what was enjoyed by society's elite was to be desired and imitated by the lower levels. Not all of polite society may have agreed with the Prince Regent's treatment of his wife and his wild ways, but ultimately he was at the very heart of their world.

There is a certain imagining of the society of Jane Austen's novels as a place of propriety and good manners, where young ladies are innocent and young men are noble; the scandalous sexualities of the Prince Regent and his upper classes are absent here. However, such a reading only scratches the surface of Austen's world; though they are all off screen, her novels are hardly without scandals: improper flirtations, secret engagements, elopements and even illegitimate

'To make herself agreeable to all'

Elizabeth receives the Darcys and Mr Bingley at Lambton. (*Pride and Prejudice*, Hugh Thomson)

children. Jane's own family was not unfamiliar with such things; Henry and Eliza's attraction and flirtation began when she was still married and her patronage from her godfather, Warren Hastings, Governor General of India, brought some to question her parentage. The Hancocks had been married for a number of years, seemingly destined to be childless, when Eliza was born. Coupled with the handsome fortune that Hastings settled upon her, rumours began to spread that Eliza was not his goddaughter, but his natural-born daughter. The rumours are never acknowledged in any of Jane's letters, but such things are certainly not ignored in her novels. In *Emma* Jane tactfully explores the place of illegitimacy within polite society in the form of Harriet Smith:

> Harriet Smith was the natural daughter of somebody. Somebody had placed her, several years back, at Mrs Goddard's school, and somebody had lately raised her from the condition of scholar to that of parlour-boarder. This was all that was generally known of her history. She had no visible friends but what had been acquired at Highbury, and was now just returned from a long visit in the country to some young ladies who had been at school there with her.

Emma, ruled by her snobbery perhaps, is convinced that Harriet must the daughter of at least a gentleman and so convinces her to refuse the farmer, Robert Martin. The more sensible Mr Knightley, however, recognises that no gentleman is likely to attach himself to illegitimacy, and that a marriage

Listening at the door.

Nancy Steele listens at the door for gossip. (*Sense and Sensibility*, Hugh Thomson)

to Robert Martin can only be an advantage to Harriet. One wonders too at the fate of Eliza, Colonel Brandon's ward in *Sense and Sensibility* and herself a product of illegitimacy, abandoned by Willoughby with his child. It is interesting, though perhaps not relevant, to note that Mr Darcy's first name and his mother's maiden name is Fitzwilliam – during the seventeenth century 'Fitz' was used to give surnames to the illegitimate children of royalty.

Scandals were social nightmares for families on any level of society, particularly if, like Mrs Bennet, they failed to contain them within their own households. Families were very much a unit when it came to Regency society, and the behaviour of one member would never fail to affect the rest. If not for Mr Darcy's forcing Mr Wickham to marry Lydia, the rest of the Bennet girls would have been ruined by her folly. When such events occurred, it was wise for families to keep it from their servants; servants in one household would often have friends and relations working in others within the same neighbourhood, and gossip would have been quickly passed from one household's maid to another and on to her mistress. Mrs Bennet, however, lacks the tact and good sense to refrain from discussing Lydia's elopement in front of her servants, and the story soon spreads across Meryton. Had she not been recovered and the situation been made as respectable as possible, her ruined reputation would have irrevocably tarnished her sisters. Much like Mr Darcy's good opinion, a good reputation lost could be lost forever. Though the Prince Regent's behaviour might suggest otherwise, Regency society had rules and boundaries. Elinor Dashwood, for example, is horrified when she learns that there was no engagement between Marianne and Mr Willoughby, despite their lack of concealment in their preference for one another. The impropriety of being so openly attached to a young man that she is not engaged to, and her manner of confronting him in London, almost destroys Marianne's reputation along with her health. Social restrictions may have allowed the judgemental hypocrisy and sneering snobbery of the likes of Caroline Bingley, but to defy them so publicly could have dire consequences for the families involved.

For what do we live, but to make sport for our neighbours, and laugh at them in our turn?

Pride and Prejudice

Charles Powett gave a dance on Thursday, to the great disturbance of all his neighbours, of course, who, you know, take a most lively interest in the state of his finances, and live in hopes of his being soon ruined.

Letter to Cassandra Austen, 1 December 1798

To be in company, nicely dressed herself and seeing others nicely dressed, to sit and smile and look pretty, and say nothing, was enough happiness for the present hour.

Emma

In all probability not an observation was made, nor an expression used by either which had not been made and used some thousands of times before, under that roof, in every Bath season, yet the merit of their being spoken with simplicity and truth, and without personal conceit, might be something uncommon.

Northanger Abbey

She would notice her; she would improve her; she would detach her from her bad acquaintance, and introduce her into good society; she would form her opinions and her manners. It would be an interesting, and certainly a very kind undertaking; highly becoming her own situation in life, her leisure, and powers.

Emma

Manners as well as appearance are, generally speaking, so totally different. Till now, I could not have supposed it possible to be mistaken as to a girl's being out or not. A girl not out has always the same sort of dress: a close bonnet, for instance; looks very demure, and never says a word.

Mansfield Park

People get so horridly poor & economical in this part of the World, that I have no patience with them. – Kent is the only place for happiness, Everybody is rich there.

Letter to Cassandra Austen, 26 December 1798

I hope we shall be in Bath in the winter; but remember, papa, if we do go, we must be in a good situation: none of your Queen-squares for us!

Persuasion

A young farmer, whether on horseback or on foot, is the very last sort of person to raise my curiosity. The yeomanry are precisely the order of people with whom I feel I can have nothing to do.

Emma

Young people will be young people, as your good mother says herself. You know I wanted you, when we first came, not to buy that sprigged muslin, but you would. Young people do not like to always be thwarted.

Northanger Abbey

People themselves alter so much, that there is something new to be observed in them for ever.

Pride and Prejudice

They could not but hold her cheap on finding that she had but two sashes, and had never learned French.

Mansfield Park

Society, I own, is necessary to me. I have been a disappointed man, and my spirits will not bear solitude.

Pride and Prejudice

This is quite the season for friendly meetings. At Christmas every body invites their friends about them, and people think little of even the worst weather.

Emma

There were more Dancers than the Room could conveniently hold, which is enough to constitute a good Ball at any time.

Letter to Cassandra Austen, 9 January 1799

It may be possible to do without dancing entirely. Instances have been known of young people passing many, many months successively, without being at any ball of any description, and no material injury accrue either to body or mind; but when a beginning is made — when the felicities of rapid motion have once been, though slightly, felt — it must be a very heavy set that does not ask for more.

Emma

There is nothing like dancing after all. I consider it as one of the first refinements of polished society.

Pride and Prejudice

I consider a country-dance as an emblem of marriage. Fidelity and complaisance are the principal duties of both; and those men who do not choose to dance or marry themselves, have no business with the partners or wives of their neighbours.

Northanger Abbey

Mr H. began with Elizabeth and afterwards danced with her again; but *they* do not know how *to be particular*. I flatter myself, however, that they will profit by the three successive lessons which I have given them.

Letter to Cassandra Austen, 9 January 1796

Dancing, I believe, like virtue, must be its own reward. Those who are standing by are usually thinking of something very different.

Emma

The Manydown Ball was a smaller thing than I expected, but it seems to have made Anna happy. At *her* age it would not have done for *me*.

Letter to Cassandra Austen, 18 January 1809

We have lived long enough in this Neighbourhood, the Basingstoke Balls are certainly on the decline, there is something interesting in the bustle of going away, & the prospect of spending future summers by the Sea or in Wales is very delightful. – For a time we shall possess many of the advantages which I have often thought of with Envy in the wives of Sailors and Soldiers.

Letter to Cassandra Austen, 3 January 1801

In marrying your nephew, I should not consider myself as quitting that sphere. He is a gentleman; I am a gentleman's daughter; so far we are equal.

Pride and Prejudice

That Lady Russell, of steady age and character, and extremely well provided for, should have no thought of a second marriage, needs no apology the public, which is rather apt to be unreasonably discontented when a women *does* marry again, than when she does *not*.

Persuasion

Lady Sondes' match surprises, but does not offend me; – had her first marriage been of affection, or had there been a single grown up daughter, I should not have forgiven her – but I consider everybody as having a right to marry *once* in their Lives for Love.

Letter to Cassandra Austen, 27 December 1808

What an alarming Bride Mrs Col Tilson must have been! Such a parade is one of the most immodest pieces of Modesty that one can imagine. To *attract* notice could have been her only wish. – It augurs ill for his family – it announces not *great* sense, & therefore ensures boundless Influence.

Letter to Cassandra Austen, 17 January 1809

Human nature is so well disposed towards those who are in interesting situations, that a young person, who either marries or dies, is sure of being kindly spoken of.

Emma

Open carriages are nasty things. A clean gown is not five minutes' wear in them. You are splashed getting in and getting out; and the wind takes your hair and your bonnet in every direction. I hate an open carriage myself.

Northanger Abbey

Surprises are foolish things. The pleasure is not enhanced, and the inconvenience is often considerable.

Emma

Before tea it was a rather dull affair; but then the before tea did not last long, for there was only one dance, danced by four couple. — Think of four couple, surrounded by an hundred people, dancing in the upper rooms at Bath!

Letter to Cassandra Austen, 12 May 1801

The young ladies who approached her at first with some respect, in consideration of her coming from a baronet's family, were soon offended by what they termed 'airs'; for, as she neither played on the pianoforte nor wore fine pelisses, they could, on farther observation, admit no right of superiority.

Mansfield Park

Mr Lyford was here yesterday; he came while we were at dinner, and partook of our elegant entertainment. I was not ashamed at asking him to sit down to table, for we had some pease-soup, a sparerib, and a pudding.

Letter to Cassandra Austen, 1 December 1798

Good company requires only birth, education, and manners, and with regard to education is not very nice. Birth and good manners are essential; but a little learning is by no means a dangerous thing in good company; on the contrary, it will do very well.

Persuasion

People are more ready to borrow & praise, than to buy – which I cannot wonder at; – but tho' I like praise as well as anybody, I like what Edward calls *Pewter* too.

Letter to Fanny Knight, 30 November 1814

The Coles were very respectable in their way, but they ought to be taught that it was not for them to arrange the terms on which the superior families would visit them.

Emma

Anne Elliot, with all her claims of birth, beauty, and mind, to throw herself away at nineteen – involve herself at nineteen in an engagement with a young man, who had nothing but himself to recommend him, and no hopes of attaining affluence but in the chances of a most uncertain profession, and no connexions to secure even his farther rise in that profession – would be, indeed, a throwing away, which she grieved to think of! Anne Elliot, so young; known to so few, to be snatched off by a stranger without alliance or fortune; or rather sunk by him into a state of most wearing, anxious, youth-killing dependence!

Persuasion

One may as well be single if the Wedding is not to be in print.

Letter to Anna Austen, February 1815

A bride, especially, is never to be neglected. More is avow-edly due to her. A bride, you know, my dear, is always the first in company, let others be who they may.

Emma

My Aunt is in a great hurry to pay me for my Cap, but cannot find in her heart to give me good money.

Letter to Cassandra Austen, 23 April 1805

We do not look in our great cities for our best morality.

Mansfield Park

The stain of illegitimacy, unbleached by nobility or wealth, would have been a stain indeed.

Emma

To be disgraced in the eye of the world, to wear the appear-ance of infamy while her heart is all purity, her actions all innocence, and the misconduct of another the true source of her debasement, is one of those circumstances which peculiarly belong to the heroine's life, and her fortitude under it what particularly dignifies her character.

Northanger Abbey

She could almost be angry herself at such angry incivility; but she checked the resentful sensation; she remembered her own ignorance. She knew not how such an offence as hers might be classed by the laws of worldly politeness, to what a degree of unforgivingness it might with propriety lead, nor to what rigours of rudeness in return it might justly make her amenable.

Northanger Abbey

These schemes are not at all the thing. Young men and women driving about the country in open carriages! Now and then it is very well, but going to inns and public places together! It is not right.

Northanger Abbey

I have been too much at my ease, too happy, too frank. I have erred against every common-place notion of decorum! I have been open and sincere where I ought to have been reserved, spiritless, dull, and deceitful. Had I talked only of the weather and the roads, and had I spoken only once in ten minutes, this reproach would have been spared.

Sense and Sensibility

The older a person grows, Harriet, the more important it is that their manners should not be bad; the more glaring and disgusting any loudness, or coarseness, or awkwardness becomes. What is passable in youth is detestable in later age.

Emma

We are each of an unsocial, taciturn disposition, unwilling to speak, unless we expect to say something that will amaze the whole room, and be handed down to posterity with all the éclat of a proverb.

Pride and Prejudice

My idea of good company, Mr. Elliot, is the company of clever, well-informed people, who have a great deal of conversation; that is what I call good company.

Persuasion

It is not time or opportunity that is to determine intimacy: — it is disposition alone. Seven years would be insufficient to make some people acquainted with each other, and seven days are more than enough for others.

Sense and Sensibility

Another stupid party last night; perhaps if larger they might be less intolerable, but here there were only just enough to make one card table, with six people to look over and talk nonsense to each other.

Letter to Cassandra Austen, 12 May 1801

There is a look of consciousness or bustle when people come in a way which they know to be beneath them.

Emma

5

LOVE & FRIENDSHIP

THOUGH JANE AUSTEN NEVER married, matrimony itself was not something she was adverse to. She happily supported the marriages of her friends and family — so she long as she thought the match a good one! Judging by her letters and novels it seems that had a proposal come from a man that Jane felt she did or could love, it would not have been unwelcome. In fact, a proposal was made in December 1802 by Harris Bigg Wither, the younger brother of Jane and Cassandra's friends Althea and Catherine Bigg. The Austen sisters were staying at Manydown House visiting their friends when Jane seems to have caught the attentions of their wealthy but rather plain and dim brother. Initially the proposal was accepted; Harris' estate would have been extensive and the marriage greatly beneficial to the Austen family. However, the engagement was to last just the one night; the following morning Jane retracted her acceptance and she and Cassandra quickly left Manydown. As to what Jane's reasons and feelings were we can only speculate, but considering opinions and advice on matrimony it's likely that she could not commit herself to a man she didn't love, no matter what his connections.

Mr Darcy makes his first proposal to Elizabeth. (*Pride and Prejudice*, Hugh Thomson)

"She is tolerable"

[Copyright 1894 by George Allen.]

Mr Darcy snubs Elizabeth as a possible dance partner. (*Pride and Prejudice*, Hugh Thomson)

Austen didn't need a love story of her own to inspire her novels. Her parents' marriage was one of mutual regard and affection, as were many of her brothers' marriages, but the story that perhaps influenced her most was that of her beloved sister Cassandra. As children, the Austens had enjoyed the company of the boys attending their father's school, including that of the Fowle brothers, from Kintbury, Berkshire. Fulwar-Craven, Tom, William and Charles Fowle, cousins to Lord Craven, would remain friends with the Austen family and Tom particularly must have been a frequent visitor to Steventon as by 1792 he and Cassandra were engaged. Their engagement, and its tragic fate, is one that Jane would later mirror in *Persuasion*, with Captain Benwick and Fanny Harville. With no money on either side there could be no marriage; Tom and Cassandra would have to wait patiently until his prospects improved enough to afford matrimony. Jane once warned one of her nieces that one must truly like a man to be willing to wait for his independence, so for Cassandra to be engaged with no hope of marrying immediately indicates what can only be described as true love. In 1795 Lord Craven offered Tom the position of chaplain to a regiment sailing to the West Indies, along with the promise of a good living on his return. Anxious to better his prospects, Tom kept his engagement a secret from his cousin and accepted the position. It was intended to be the change in his fortune, and on his return he would be able to finally wed Cassandra. But no such happiness was to come from the voyage: in February 1797, as he was due to return to England in the May, Tom caught a fever and died in St Domingo. Cassandra, who had perhaps by now been preparing for her wedding, was left heartbroken and devastated. Sensible Tom had drafted a will before the journey, leaving Cassandra with a sum of £1,000. It would be a welcome relief in the hard times after Mr Austen's death, but it was hardly enough for a single woman to survive on. Yet Cassandra, though still in her twenties and in possession of her looks, never entertained the prospect of another match and devoted herself instead to her role as sister and aunt.

Death was an ever-present danger when it came to love in the Regency period. Brief, unexplained maladies often claimed the lives of the otherwise young and healthy, and childbirth was an unpredictable, risky venture. The Austen brothers were no stranger to such tragedies; both Edward's wife Elizabeth and Frank's Mary died after giving birth to their eleventh child, and Charles' wife Harriet died delivering her fourth.

Tragedies were not to be the Austens' only experiences of love, however, and Jane delighted in the lives and loves of her two eldest nieces, James' Anna and Edward's Fanny. Though both girls were born in 1793, their lives and characters were worlds apart but both enjoyed a close friendship with their Aunt Jane.

Though Fanny had been born in January, Kent was too far from Steventon for the Austens to have much involvement. Deane parsonage, however, was within walking distance and Anna's birth in the April was reportedly attended by

Mr Willoughby takes an illicit lock of Marianne's hair. (*Sense and Sensibility*, Hugh Thomson)

Mrs Austen, who trampled across the countryside in the middle of the night to help her daughter-in-law. After the death of her mother in 1795, little Jane Anna Elizabeth Austen was sent by her mourning father from Deane to neighbouring Steventon, to be cared for by her grandmother. Her Aunt Jane, who would have been almost 20 years old, became quite attached to the little girl during her stay. Anna's return to Deane after her father's marriage to Mary Lloyd would not be a smooth one; after the vibrancy of her clever Aunt Jane and the warmth of Steventon, Anna was less than pleased with her new stepmother. Even after the birth of her half-siblings, Anna much preferred the company of her witty aunt and charming uncles, as well as the home of the grandparents who adored her. As she grew older, her lively, sensitive spirit continued to clash with her stepmother's and her behaviour became increasingly difficult. One family tale tells of Anna, who perhaps felt neglected by her father, defiantly cutting off her hair, and at 16 she engaged herself to a man in his thirties, only to break it off once her father had given his permission.

Unable, or perhaps or unwilling, to deal with his daughter's behaviour, James sent Anna to her grandmother and aunts, who were now at Chawton. Though Anna's months at the cottage in 1810 were intended as punishment, she was more a welcome guest than a disgraced exile. Anna might not have known it at the time, but Jane must have been redrafting *Sense and Sensibility* and perhaps even *Pride and Prejudice*. Though she was initially unaware of her aunt's publication – the secret seems to have been revealed a few months after

Sense and Sensibility was printed – Anna knew Jane to be a talented writer, something she both admired and aspired to. In 1814, Jane's letters to her Anna were full of advice and support for her niece's own literary endeavours. In a letter dated 9 September, Jane praised Anna's progress with her manuscript and its subject manor; it is perhaps interesting to note that Austen would have begun work on *Emma* around this time:

> You are now collecting your people delightfully, getting them exactly into such a spot as is the delight of my life. Three or four families in a country village is the very thing to work on, and I hope you will do a great deal more, and make full use of them while they are so very favourably arranged.

The year 1814 would also see Anna Austen become a bride after a more proper engagement, this time to Benjamin Lefroy, the son of Aunt Jane's friend and mentor Madame Lefroy. Her sister Caroline, then 9 years old, would remember their wedding as a quiet, colourless affair with very few of the family present. But a Regency wedding was rarely grand, as Austen reveals in *Emma*:

> The wedding was very much like other weddings, where the parties have no taste for finery or parade; and Mrs Elton, from the particulars detailed by her husband, thought it all extremely shabby, and very inferior to her own. 'Very little white satin, very few lace veils; a most pitiful business!'

By assigning such thoughts to Mrs Elton, silly and material, Jane indicates that a respectable wedding would have been simple one. And was Anna's marriage a respectable one? The impetuous, unsteady nature of her youth certainly seems to have calmed after she became Mrs Lefroy. Though Anna never published, she continued to write even after her marriage and motherhood, and even attempted to continue her aunt's unfinished manuscript, *Sanditon*.

Whilst 15-year-old Anna was wild and impulsive in Hampshire, in Kent her cousin Fanny found herself and her ten younger siblings motherless. Elizabeth's death left her husband grief-stricken and Jane recognised that it would fall to Fanny to support him:

> Dearest Fanny must now look upon her-self as his prime source of comfort, his dearest friend; as the being who is gradually to supply to him, to the extent that is possible, what he has lost. This consideration will elevate and cheer her.

Cassandra had fortunately been staying at Godmersham to help Elizabeth in her eleventh confinement, but could not stay to support her niece forever. Her world now seems further from her cousin Anna's than ever; as the eldest daughter the role of mistress of Godmersham, and of mother, would now belong to Fanny. She bore her new fate well, becoming such a steady and

Placed it before Anne.

Wentworth leaves a letter expressing his feelings for Anne. (*Persuasion*, Hugh Thomson)

affectionate companion to her father that one wonders if Austen used her for inspiration in creating Emma Woodhouse.

Whilst Anna's letters sought literary guidance, Fanny's begged her aunt's opinion on matters of the heart. With no mother to guide her, Fanny relied on her Aunt Jane's judgement when it came to vetting potential husbands. As the daughter of a man like Edward Austen Knight, with such fortune and property, Fanny must have been an attractive potential wife. The tone of Jane's replies is playful and affectionate; she is evidently amused and entertained by her niece's dilemmas of the heart, perhaps transported back to her own flirtatious youth. Despite this, the advice that Austen provided Fanny is sound and supportive, encouraging her against making any hasty engagements at so young an age. Fanny heeded her Aunt Jane's advice; she did not marry until 1820, by which time she was 27 years old. Her husband was a wealthy widower, Sir Edward Knatchbull, who already had six children – would Jane have approved of him? Perhaps not. Despite his status Knatchbull was reportedly overbearing and extremely conservative, hardly the sort of gentleman Austen must have dreamed of for her favourite niece. The couple would have nine children together and Lady Knatchbull would outlive her husband by more than thirty years.

Friendship is certainly the finest balm for the pangs of disappointed love.

Northanger Abbey

Miss Fletcher and I were very thick, but I am the thinnest of the two.

Letter to Cassandra Austen, 15 January 1796

I often think ... that there is nothing so bad as parting with one's friends. One seems quite forlorn without them.

Pride and Prejudice

There is nothing I would not do for those who are really my friends. I have no notion of loving people by halves; it is not in my nature. My attachments are always excessively strong.

Northanger Abbey

My dear, pray do not make any more matches; they are silly things, and break up one's family circle grievously.

Emma

The Admiral hated marriage, and thought it never pardonable in a young man of independent fortune.

Mansfield Park

That expression of 'violently in love' is so hackneyed, so doubtful, so indefinite, that it gives me very little idea. It is often applied to feelings which arise from a half-hour's acquaintance, as to a real, strong attachment.

Pride and Prejudice

Matrimony, as the origin of change, was always disagreeable.

Emma

I only do not like you should marry anybody. And yet I do wish you to marry very much, because I know you will never be happy till you are; but the loss of a Fanny Knight will be never made up to me; My 'affec: Niece F.C. Wildman' will be but a poor Substitute.

Letter to Fanny Knight, 20 February 1817

I wonder who first discovered the efficacy of poetry in driving away love!

Pride and Prejudice

I have none of the usual inducements of women to marry. Were I to fall in love, indeed, it would be a different thing! but I have never been in love; it is not my way, or my nature; and I do not think I ever shall.

Emma

Nothing could be more delightful! To be fond of dancing was a certain step towards falling in love.

Pride and Prejudice

Thank you; for now we shall soon be acquainted, as I am authorized to tease you on this subject whenever we meet, and nothing in the world advances intimacy so much.

Northanger Abbey

I am almost afraid to tell you how my Irish friend and I behaved. Imagine to yourself everything most profligate and shocking in the way of dancing and sitting down together.

Letter to Cassandra Austen, 9 January 1796

This sensation of listlessness, weariness, stupidity, this disinclination to sit down and employ myself, this feeling of every thing's being dull and insipid about the house! – I must be in love; I should be the oddest creature in the world if I were not.

Emma

I am now convinced, my dear aunt, that I have never been much in love; for had I really experienced that pure and elevating passion, I should at present detest his very name, and wish him all manner of evil. But my feelings are not only cordial towards him; they are even impartial towards Miss King. I cannot find out that I hate her at all, or that I am in the least unwilling to think her a very good sort of girl. There can be no love in all this. My watchfulness has been effectual; and though I should certainly be a more interesting object to all my acquaintance, were I distractedly in love with him.

Pride and Prejudice

I have no scruple in saying that you cannot be in Love. My dear Fanny, I am ready to laugh at the idea – and yet it is no laughing matter to have had you so mistaken as to your own feelings – And with all my heart I wish I had cautioned you on that point when first you spoke to me.

Letter to Fanny Knight, 18 November 1814

Next to being married, a girl likes to be crossed a little in love now and then.

Pride and Prejudice

Mr Rushworth was from the first struck with the beauty of Miss Bertram, and, being inclined to marry, soon fancied himself in love.

Mansfield Park

I am, Sophia, quite ready to make a foolish match. Any body between fifteen and thirty may have me for asking. A little beauty, and a few smiles, and a few compliments to the navy, and I am a lost man.

Persuasion

I would have everybody marry if they can do it properly: I do not like to have people throw themselves away; but everybody should marry as soon as they can do it to advantage.

Mansfield Park

When I consider how few young Men you have yet seen much of – how capable you are (yes, I do still think you *very* capable) of being really in love – and how full of temptation the next 6 or 7 years of your Life will probably be – (it is the very period of Life for the *strongest* attachments to be formed).

Letter to Fanny Knight, 30 November 1814

I hate the idea of one great fortune looking out for another. And to marry for money I think the wickedest thing in existence.

Northanger Abbey

He wanted to marry well, and having the arrogance to raise his eyes to her, pretended to be in love; but she was perfectly easy as to his not suffering ay disappointment that need be cared for. There had been no real affection either in language or manners.

Emma

Being now in her twenty-first year, Maria Bertram was beginning to think matrimony a duty; and as a marriage with Mr Rushworth would give her the enjoyment of a larger income than her father's, as well as ensure her the house in town, which was now a prime object, it became, by the same rule of moral obligation, her evident duty to marry Mr Rushworth if she could.

Mansfield Park

My being charming, Harriet, is not quite enough to induce me to marry, I must find other people charming – one other person at least.

Emma

It was a very proper wedding. The bride was elegantly dressed; the two bridesmaids were duly inferior; her father gave her away; her mother stood with salts in her hand, expecting to be agitated; her aunt tried to cry; and the service was impressively read by Dr. Grant. Nothing could be objected to.

Mansfield Park

It must very improper that a young lady should dream of a gentleman before the gentleman is first known to have dreamt of her.

Northanger Abbey

The gentleness and gratitude of her disposition would secure her all your own immediately. From my soul I do not think she would marry you *without* love; that is, if there is a girl in the world capable of being uninfluenced by ambition, I can suppose it her; but ask her to love you, and she will never have the heart to refuse.

Mansfield Park

Anne hoped she had outlived the age of blushing; but the age of emotion she certainly had not.

Persuasion

There is no charm equal to tenderness of heart ... There is nothing to be compared with it. Warmth and tenderness of heart, with an affectionate, open manner, will beat all the clearness of head in the world.

Emma

He was in love, very much in love; and it was a love which, operating on an active, sanguine spirit, of more warmth than delicacy, made her affection appear of greater consequence because it was withheld, and determined him to have the glory, as well as the felicity, of forcing her to love him.

Mansfield Park

I must confess, my vanity only was elevated by it. Careless of her happiness, thinking only of my own amusement, giving way to feelings which I had always been too much in the habit of indulging, I endeavoured, by every means in my power, to make myself pleasing to her, without any design of returning her affection.

Sense and Sensibility

This it is, her not caring about you, which gives her such a soft skin, and makes her so much taller, and produces all these charms and graces! I do desire that you will not be making her really unhappy; a *little* love, perhaps, may animate and do her good, but I will not have you plunge her deep, for she is as good a little creature as ever lived, and has a great deal of feeling.

Mansfield Park

She had feeling, genuine feelings. It would be something to be loved by such a girl, to excite the first ardours of her young unsophisticated mind!

Mansfield Park

Love such as his, in a man like himself, must with perseverance secure a return, and at no great distance; and he had so much delight in the idea of obliging her to love him in a very short time, that her not loving him now was scarcely regretted. A little difficulty to be overcome was no evil to Henry Crawford. He rather derived spirits from it. He had been apt to gain hearts too easily. His situation was new and animating.

Mansfield Park

I was tempted by his attentions and allowed myself to appear pleased. An old story, probably – a common case – and no more than has happened to hundreds of my sex before; and yet it may not be the more excusable in one who sets up as I do for understanding.

Emma

The struggle was great – but it ended too soon. My affection for Marianne, my thorough conviction of her attachment to me – it was all insufficient to outweigh that dread of poverty, or get the better of those false ideas of the necessity of riches, which I was naturally inclined to feel.

Sense and Sensibility

Years may pass, before he is Independent. —You like him well enough to marry, but not well enough to wait. —The unpleasantness of appearing fickle is certainly great.

Letter to Fanny Knight, 30 November 1814

In vain I have struggled. It will not do. My feelings will not be repressed. You must allow me to tell you how ardently I admire and love you.

Pride and Prejudice

If I loved you less, I might be able to talk about it more.

Emma

A few months had seen the beginning and the end of their acquaintance; but, not with a few months ended Anne's share of suffering from it. Her attachment and regrets had, for a long time, clouded every enjoyment of youth; and an early loss of bloom and spirits had been their lasting effect.

Persuasion

She had no hope, nothing to deserve in the name of hope, that he could have that sort of affection for herself which was now in question.

Emma

Never had she so honestly felt that she could have loved him, as now, when all love must be vain.

Pride and Prejudice

Marianne could never love by halves; and her whole heart became, in time, as much devoted to her husband, as it had once been to Willoughby.

Sense and Sensibility

Oh, Lizzy! do anything rather than marry without affection. Are you quite sure that you feel what you ought to do?

Pride and Prejudice

Nothing can be compared to the misery of being bound *without* Love, bound to one, & preferring another. *That* is a Punishment which you do *not* deserve.

Letter to Fanny Knight, 30 November 1814

I have not a doubt of your doing very well together. Your tempers are by no means unlike. You are each of you so complying, that nothing will ever be resolved on; so easy, that every servant will cheat you; and so generous, that you will always exceed your income.

Pride and Prejudice

It was a union of the highest promise of felicity in itself, and without one real, rational difficulty to oppose or delay it.

Emma

'I do, I do like him,' she replied, with tears in her eyes, 'I love him. Indeed he has no improper pride. He is perfectly amiable. You do not know what he really is; then pray do not pain me by speaking of him in such terms.'

Pride and Prejudice

Half the sum of attraction, on either side, might have been enough, for he had nothing to do, and she had hardly any body to love; but the encounter of such lavish recommendations could not fail. They were gradually acquainted, and when acquainted, rapidly and deeply in love.

Persuasion

She began now to comprehend that he was exactly the man who, in disposition and talents, would most suit her. His understanding and temper, though unlike her own, would have answered all her wishes. It was an union that must have been to the advantage of both; by her ease and liveliness, his mind might have been softened, his manners improved, and from his judgment, information, and knowledge of the world, she must have received benefit of greater importance.

Pride and Prejudice

A few minutes were sufficient for making her acquainted with her own heart. A mind like hers; once opening to suspicion, made rapid progress; she touched, she admitted, she acknowledged the whole truth ... It darted through her, with the speed of an arrow, that Mr Knightley must marry no one but herself!

Emma

Marianne Dashwood was born to an extraordinary fate. She was born to discover the falsehood of her own opinions, and to counteract, by her conduct, her most favourite maxims. She was born to overcome an affection formed so late in life as at seventeen, and with no sentiment superior to strong esteem and lively friendship, voluntarily to give her hand to another! – and *that* other, a man who had suffered no less than herself under the event of a former attachment, – whom, two years before, she had considered too old to be married, – and who still sought the constitutional safeguard of a flannel waistcoat!

Sense and Sensibility

Henry was now sincerely attached to her, though he felt and delighted in all the excellencies of her character and truly loved her society, I must confess that his affection originated in nothing better than gratitude, or, in other words, that a persuasion of her partiality for him had been the only cause of giving her a serious thought. It is a new circumstance in romance, I acknowledge, and dreadfully derogatory of an heroine's dignity; but if it be as new in common life, the credit of a wild imagination will at least be all my own.

Northanger Abbey

The happiness which this reply produced, was such as he had probably never felt before; and he expressed himself on the occasion as sensibly and as warmly as a man violently in love can be supposed to do. Had Elizabeth been able to encounter his eye, she might have seen how well the expression of heartfelt delight, diffused over his face, became him; but, though she could not look, she could listen, and he told her of feelings, which, in proving of what importance she was to him, made his affection every moment more valuable.

Pride and Prejudice

You pierce my soul. I am half agony, half hope. Tell me not that I am too late, that such precious feelings are gone for ever. I offer myself to you again with a heart even more your own than when you almost broke it, eight and a half years ago. Dare not say that a man forgets sooner than woman, that his love has an earlier death. I have loved none but you. Unjust I may have been, weak and resentful I have been, but never inconstant.

Persuasion

With so much true merit and true love, and no want of fortune and friends, the happiness of the married cousins must appear as secure as earthly happiness can be.

Mansfield Park

To begin perfect happiness at the respective ages of twenty-six and eighteen is to do pretty well; and professing myself moreover convinced that the general's unjust interference, so far from being really injurious to their felicity, was perhaps rather conducive to it, by improving their knowledge of each other, and adding strength to their attachment, I leave it to be settled, by whomsoever it may concern, whether the tendency of this work be altogether to recommend parental tyranny, or reward filial disobedience.

Northanger Abbey

Perhaps it is our imperfections that make us so perfect for one another!

Emma

I cannot fix on the hour, or the spot, or the look, or the words, which laid the foundation. It is too long ago. I was in the middle before I knew that I had begun.

Pride and Prejudice

Who can be in doubt of what followed? When any two young people take it into their heads to marry, they are pretty sure by perseverance to carry their point, be they ever so poor, or ever so imprudent, or ever so little likely to be necessary to each other's ultimate comfort. This may be bad morality to conclude with, but I believe it to be truth; and if such parties succeed, how should a Captain Wentworth and an Anne Elliot, with the advantage of maturity of mind, consciousness of right, and one independent fortune between them, fail of bearing down every opposition?

Persuasion

6

READING & WRITING

As the ranks of the middle classes swelled and multiplied at the end of the eighteenth century, so too did the levels of literacy amongst young women. To be able to read and write well was an important part of girls being considered refined; letter writing in particular came to be considered as one of the great female accomplishments. An elegant hand indicated an elegant mind, and a girl who was a devoted, capable correspondent would always be thought well of. Letter writing was crucial for women in the Regency period. Without the ability to travel freely, letters were vital to maintain acquaintances and to remain up to date with the goings on at home and abroad. Indeed, the life of a young lady at the turn of the century could hardly have been fulfilling. Their quaint country lives and their feminine occupations have been somewhat romanticised by the twenty-first-century media: it is imagined as a simpler time, of polite society and elegant manners. In reality, without needlework, music and art young ladies would have found their days uncomfortably empty. Lacking the independence of their brothers to attend university, travel as they pleased or pursue a career, letter writing provided single women with constant occupation. The frequency of letters from Jane to Cassandra Austen, some begun by Jane knowing her sister could not yet have received the previous, suggests that reading and answering one's correspondence would have been a daily task. Letters also provided small country societies with points of conversation: the news

"Marianne, wrapped up in her own music"

The romantic Marianne takes solace at the piano. (*Sense and Sensibility*, Chris Hammond)

received in a letter must be relayed to family and friends so that their observations and opinions may be recorded in the reply. Indeed, letter writing in the Regency was not quite as private as we might imagine. Letters were read aloud or passed around, particularly if it was from an intended spouse or a yet unseen addition to the social circle, so that the hand-writing might be scrutinised and the tone examined.

Of course, letters were also a place to express what a person could not express vocally, as is the case with both Mr Darcy and Captain Wentworth. The matter of Georgiana's near ruin at the hand of Mr Wickham is too sensitive for con-versation; it requires the time and consideration of expression that only a letter can offer. Captain Wentworth similarly requires the use of a pen to convey his emotions:

I can listen no longer in silence. I must speak to you by such means as are within my reach. You pierce my soul. I am half agony, half hope. Tell me not that I am too late, that such precious feelings are gone for ever. I offer myself to you again with a heart even more your own than when you almost broke it, eight years and a half ago. Dare not say that man forgets sooner than woman, that his love has an earlier death. I have loved none but you. Unjust I may have been, weak and resentful I have been, but never inconstant. You alone have brought me to Bath. For you alone, I think and plan. Have you not seen this? Can you fail to have understood my wishes? I had not waited even these ten days, could I have read your feelings, as I think you must have penetrated mine. I can hardly write. I am every instant hearing something which overpowers me. You sink your voice, but I can distinguish the tones of that voice when they would be lost on others. Too good, too excellent creature! You do us justice, indeed. You do believe that there is true attachment and constancy among men. Believe it to be most fervent, most undeviating, in F. W.

For men like Captain Wentworth, and perhaps particularly Mr Darcy, pride and propriety makes such expression difficult – as Mr Knightley tells Emma, 'If I loved you less, I might be able to talk about it more'. Of course, letters also allow the recipient of such emotions the power of re-reading, of analysing and considering them in way that a verbal confession would not permit.

Letter writing would not be the only tool at disposal of a young lady in need of entertainment. The rise in literacy levels was accompanied by an increase in the popularity of the novel. Even by the Regency, the novel was still a fairly new art form and one with a mixed reputation. Some belittled it as frivolous, lacking the seriousness of a history or the skill of a poem, whilst others condemned them as scandalous and immoral. In her defence of the novel in *Northanger Abbey*, Austen defends the novel's legitimacy as an art form, proving that even at the end of the eighteenth century its reputation was still dubious:

'My father is come!'

The play at Mansfield Park is interrupted by the return of Sir Thomas.
(*Mansfield Park*, Hugh Thomson)

The greatest powers of the mind are displayed, in which the most thorough knowledge of human nature, the happiest delineation of its varieties, the liveliest effusions of wit and humour, are conveyed to the world in the best-chosen language.

In the same chapter, John Thorpe dismisses novels because he perceives them as too silly and feminine; they are for his sisters, not for him. Novels had become something of a female occupation, though there is a feeling in Austen that not everybody in society thought it an attractive one. Miss Bingley attempts to mock Elizabeth for her preference for books over cards (yet when she later observes Mr Darcy reading she professes to love reading herself):

On entering the drawing-room she found the whole party at loo, and was immediately invited to join them; but suspecting them to be playing high, she declined it, for the short time she could stay below, with a book. Mr. Hurst looked at her with astonishment.

'Do you prefer reading to cards?' said he; 'that is rather singular.'

'Miss Eliza Bennet,' said Miss Bingley, 'despises cards. She is a great reader, and has no pleasure in anything else.'

Novels, particularly the Gothic romances adored by Catherine Morland, did perhaps have more allure for women than they did for men. Just as letter writing afforded them the power to maintain and enjoy societies they did not have the ability to attend, in a novel travel, romance and even scandal could all be experienced from the safety of their fathers' homes. However, this was not without its dangers; in *Northanger Abbey* Austen scolds Catherine for forming her expectations on the far-fetched adventures of Emily St Aubert, heroine of *The Mysteries of Udolpho*. What she does promote, however, is a readership like Henry Tilney's, who is able to greatly enjoy the novel (one of the indicators of his superiority to John Thorpe) but appreciate it for what it is: a story. Of course, not all novels were to be treated like the Gothic romances. Writers like Samuel Richardson, whose moral epic *Clarissa* was a key player in legitimising the novel, actually published with the hope and intention that young ladies would learn from them. Austen was a great admirer of Richardson, whose novel *Sir Charles Grandison* was one of her favourites and her early writing borrowed much in style and form from Richardson's work. Richardson, like another of Austen's favourite novelists the satirist Fanny Burney, used the extremely popular method of writing novels as a series of letters between the characters, known as an 'epistolary'. Two pieces of Austen's juvenilia, *Love and Freinship* [sic] and *Lady Susan*, are penned in this style, as was the earliest version of *Sense and Sensibility*, called *Elinor and Marianne*. Though she would eventually abandon the epistolary form, the influence of both Richardson and Burney is still visible in the social satire Austen uses to express her opinions in the completed novels.

Jane Austen's introduction to these writers would have been early encouraged by her father and his extensive library. The Austen family were great readers, and Jane's letters reveal that the acquisition of a new novel was an exciting event at Steventon. Novels were read both alone and with family, taking it in turns to read chapters aloud to one another. At Steventon, literary pursuits were to be nurtured and encouraged and by 11 years old Jane had already begun to fancy herself a writer. Like the novels in her father's collection, these early stories were to be enjoyed by her family. Whether or not they were written for specific events is unclear, but pieces were dedicated to Francis and Charles on their entering the navy and the births of both Fanny and Anna were commemorated with dedications too. These short stories were wonderfully ridiculous, bawdy satires that are just what one would expect from a teenage Jane Austen. The cult of sensibility is ridiculed often, but particularly in *Love and Freinship* [sic] – the piece's breathless pace and wildly improbable events are an early attack on the novels she would mock again in *Northanger Abbey*. The juvenile Austen thinks little of these helpless young ladies who faint and swoon, and even less of their hasty attachments and ill-advised marriages. But the heroines of sensibility were not her only target. Her later novella, *Lady Susan*, written around the age of 19, chronicles the schemes and subsequent downfall of a beautiful, manipulative widow. The character of Lady Susan Vernon herself is remarkable, and unlike anyone found in Austen's later novels; she is a consciously bad mother, preferring to use her daughter as a pawn in her great game of social chess, and an undeniably sexual woman. There is little subtlety here: that Lady Susan has had affairs is evident and her pursuit of Reginald de Courcy is almost predatory.

After *Lady Susan* Jane Austen began to develop her skills as a novelist, beginning work on *Elinor and Marianne* in her early twenties. Her writing was both enjoyed and encouraged by her family, in particular by her father. He must have seen the talent in his daughter's early manuscripts, because he wrote to the publisher Thomas Cadell offering the first draft of *Pride and Prejudice*, *First Impressions*:

Sir,

I have in my possession a manuscript novel, comprising 3 vols., about the length of Miss Burney's Evelina. As I am well aware of what consequence it is that a work of this sort should make its first appearance under a respectable name, I apply to you. I shall be much obliged, therefore, if you will inform me whether you choose to be concerned in it, what will be the expense of publishing it at the author's risk, and what you will venture to advance for the property of it, if on perusal it is approved of. Should you give any encouragement, I will send you the work.

I am, Sir, your humble servant,

GEORGE AUSTEN

Cadell of course declined the offer, returning the letter 'declined by returned of post'. It must have been a sad shame for George Austen, but for his daughter's fans it has been a blessing: had Cadell accepted the novel in 1797 it would never have become *Pride and Prejudice*.

Austen's first chance at publication came in 1803, when her brother Henry helped her to sell a manuscript entitled

Susan to Crosby and Co. for the sum of £10. The family waited patiently for the novel's publication, but Jane's *Susan* never appeared. In 1809, settled now at Chawton Cottage, Austen wrote to enquire after the state of her work, amusingly signing the letter as Mrs Ashton Dennis:

Gentlemen

In the spring of the year of 1808, a MS Novel in 2 vol. entitled Susan was sold to you by a Gentleman of the name of Seymour, & the purchase money £10 rec'd at the same time. Six years have since passed, & this work of which I am myself the Authoress, has never to the best of my knowledge, appeared in print, tho' an early publication was stipulated for at the time of sale. I can only account for such an extraordinary circumstance by supposing the MS by some carelessness to have been lost; & if that was the case, am willing to supply you with another copy if you are disposed to avail yourselves of it, & will engage for no farther delay when it comes into your hands. It will not be in my power from particular circumstances to command this copy before the Month of August, but then, if you accept my proposal, you may depend on receiving it. Be so good as to send me a Line in answer as soon as possible, as my stay in this place will not exceed a few days. Should no notice be taken of this address, I shall feel myself at liberty to secure the publication of my work, by applying elsewhere. I am Gentleman &c. &c.

M.A.D.

Crosby may have decided not to publish the novel, but he had purchased it fairly and if Jane wanted it, she would have to pay. For a woman on such a limited income as Jane Austen's this would have been almost impossible and *Susan* was not retrieved until the profits from *Sense and Sensibility* in 1811 and *Pride and Prejudice* in 1813 could afford to bring her home. After their long separation, Jane set to work updating and editing the manuscript, which included changing the heroine's name to Catherine Morland. Poor Jane never would see the novel she had pinned all her early hopes on published, as both *Northanger Abbey*, as it became, and *Persuasion* were published after her death by Henry and Cassandra.

Where shall I begin? Which of all my important nothings shall I tell you first?

Letter to Cassandra Austen, 15 June 1808

The person, be it gentleman or lady, who has not pleasure in a good novel must be intolerably suited.

Northanger Abbey

I declare there is no enjoyment like reading! How much sooner one tires of anything else than of a book!

Pride and Prejudice

From fifteen to seventeen she was in training for a heroine; she read all such works as heroines must read to supply their memories with those quotations which are so serviceable and so soothing in the vicissitudes of their eventful lives.

Northanger Abbey

Marianne, who had the knack of finding her way in every house to the library, however it might be avoided by the family in general, soon procured herself a book.

Sense and Sensibility

Yes, novels; – for I will not adopt that ungenerous and impolitic custom so common with novel-writers, of degrading by their contemptuous censure the very performances, to the number of which they are themselves adding – joining with their greatest enemies in bestowing the harshest epithets on such works, and scarcely ever permitting them to be read by their own heroine, who, if she accidentally take up a novel, is sure to turn over its insipid pages with disgust. Alas! if the heroine of one novel be not patronized by the heroine of another, from whom can she expect protection and regard? I cannot approve of it.

Northanger Abbey

'Oh! it is only a novel!' replies the young lady, while she lays down her book with affected indifference, or momentary shame. 'It is only *Cecilia*, or *Camilla*, or *Belinda*'; or, in short, only some work in which the greatest powers of the mind are displayed, in which the most thorough knowledge of human nature, the happiest delineation of its varieties, the liveliest effusions of wit and humour, are conveyed to the world in the best-chosen language.

Northanger Abbey

She thought it was the misfortune of poetry to be seldom safely enjoyed by those who enjoyed it completely; and that the strong feelings which alone could estimate it truly were the very feelings which ought to taste it but sparingly.

Persuasion

Novels are all so full of nonsense and stuff; there has not been a tolerably decent one come out since Tom Jones, except The Monk; I have read that t'other day; but as for all the others, they are stupidest things in creation.

Northanger Abbey

To set against your new Novel, of which nobody ever heard before & perhaps never may again, We have got *Ida of Athens* by Miss Owenson; which must be very clever, because it was written as the Authoress says, in three months.

Letter to Cassandra Austen, 17 January 1809

The anxiety, which in this state of their attachment must be the portion of Henry and Catherine, and of all who loved either, as to its final event, can hardly extend, I fear, to the bosom of my readers, who will see in the tell-tale compression of the pages before them, that we are all hastening together to perfect felicity.

Northanger Abbey

Indeed, I *do* think you get on very fast. I wish other people of my acquaintance could compose so rapidly.

Letter to Anna Austen, 30 November 1814

The letter I have received from you has diverted me beyond moderation. I could die of laughter at it, as they used to say at school. You are indeed the finest comic writer of the present age.

Letter to Cassandra Austen, 1 January 1796

Letters are no matter of indifference they are generally a very positive curse.

Emma

You are inimitable, irresistible. You are the delight of my Life. Such Letters, such entertaining Letters as you have lately sent! – Such a description of your queer little heart! – Such a lovely display of what Imagination does.

Letter to Fanny Knight, 20 February 1817

I have written to Mrs E. Leigh too, and Mrs Heathcote has been ill-natured enough to send me a letter of enquiry; so that altogether I am tolerably tired of letter writing.

Letter to Cassandra Austen, 25 November 1796

Everybody allows that the talent of writing agreeable letters is particularly female.

Northanger Abbey

I am sure nobody can desire your letters so much as I do, and I don't think anybody deserves them so well.

Letter to Cassandra Austen, 25 November 1796

Nothing could be more delicious than your Letter; & the assurance of your feeling relieved by writing it, made the pleasure perfect.

Letter to Fanny Knight, 13 March 1817

To make long sentences upon unpleasant subjects is very odious, & I shall therefore get rid of the one now uppermost in my thoughts as soon as possible.

Letter to Cassandra Austen, 25 May 1801

It is a rule with me, that a person who can write a long letter with ease, cannot write ill.

Pride and Prejudice

There, I flatter myself I have constructed you a Smartish
Letter, considering my want of Materials. But like my
dear Dr Johnson I believe I have dealt more with Notions
than Facts.

> Letter to Cassandra Austen, 8 February 1807

As you have by this time received my last letter, it is fit that
I should begin another.

> Letter to Cassandra Austen, 3 January 1801

I am very flattered by your commendation of my last
Letter, for I write only for Fame, and without any view to
pecuniary Emolument.

> Letter to Cassandra Austen, 14 January 1796

My Letter was a scratch of a note compared with yours
– & then you write so even, so clear both in style &
Penmanship, so much to the point & give so much real
intelligence that is enough to kill one.

> Letter to Francis Austen, 25 September 1813

Let other pens dwell on guilt and misery. I quit such odious
subjects as soon as I can, impatient to restore everybody,
not greatly in fault themselves, to tolerable comfort, and
to have done with all the rest.

> *Mansfield Park*

What should I do your strong, manly, spirited Sketches, full of Variety & Glow? – How could I possibly join them on to the little bit (two inches wide) of Ivory on which I work with so fine a Brush, as produces little effect after much labour?

Letter to James Edward Austen Leigh, 16 December 1816

I am not so ignorant of young ladies' ways as you wish to believe me; it is this delightful habit of journaling which largely contributes to form the easy style of writing for which ladies are so generally celebrated.

Northanger Abbey

I could not sit seriously down to write a serious Romance under any other motive than to save my Life, & if it were indispensable for me to keep it up & never relax into laughing at myself or other people, I am sure I should be hung before I had finished the first Chapter.

Letter to James Stanier Clarke, 1 April 1816

I am gratified by her having pleasure in what I write – but I wish the knowledge of my being exposed to her discerning Criticism, may not hurt my stile, by inducing too great a solitude. I begin already to weigh my words & sentences more than I did, & am looking about for sentiment, an illustration or a metaphor in every corner of the room. Could my Ideas flow as fast as the rain in the Storecloset, it would be charming.

Letter to Cassandra Austen, 24 January 1809

No indeed, I am never too busy to think of [*Sense and Sensibility*]. I can no more forget it, than a mother can forget her suckling child.

Letter to Cassandra Austen, 25 April 1811

She really does seem to admire Elizabeth [Bennet]. I must confess *I* think her as the delightful a creature as ever appeared in print, & how I shall be able to tolerate those do not like *her* at least, I do not know.

Letter to Cassandra Austen, 29 January 1813

Henry & I went to the Exhibition in Spring Gardens. It is not thought a good collection, but I was very well pleased – particularly (pray tell Fanny) with a small portrait of Mrs Bingley, excessively like her. I went in hopes of seeing one of her Sister, but there was no Mrs Darcy.

Letter to Cassandra Austen, 24 May 1813

I have been very much entertained by your story of Carolina & her aged Father, it made me laugh heartily, & I am particularly glad to find you so much alive upon any topic of such absurdity.

Letter to Caroline Austen, 15 July 1816

I have now attained the true art of letter-writing, which we are always told is to express on paper exactly what one would say to the same person by word of mouth. I have been talking to you almost as fast as I could the whole of this letter.

Letter to Cassandra Austen, 3 January 1801

7

WIT & WISDOM

WHEN JANE AUSTEN WROTE *Northanger Abbey* it was not only to satirise the ridiculous nature of early Gothic novels. In her mockery and witticisms, Austen's intention was not just for humour but to educate the number of young women who idolised its heroines. As the narrator, Jane ridicules those whose behaviour and ideals she deems shallow, irrational or simply silly. Throughout her work she warns against short acquaintances and impulsive marriages, as well as the pitfalls of vanity, arrogance and poor judgment. Her comments on society to her sister Cassandra and her letters of advice to her niece Fanny reveal a side of Jane that was deeply concerned with the behaviour of others.

Considering *Northanger Abbey*'s function as a parody – and, therefore, a critique of that mode of behaviour – we can assume that Jane Austen was acutely aware of the way in which young women like Catherine Morland read novels. The sheltered lives of these educated, middle-class young women offered them little experience when it came to the society of towns like Bath and London. For such girls, novels were their

Soon made her quick eye sufficiently acquainted with
Mr. Robert Martin

Emma disapproves of Harriet's acquaintance with Robert Martin.
(*Emma*, Chris Hammond)

Sitting under trees with Fanny.

Edmund and Fanny sit beneath the trees. (*Mansfield Park*, Hugh Thomson)

only connection with the world beyond their villages, and so novels became the basis for their expectations of society as well as the model for their conduct. *Northanger Abbey*, along with *Sense and Sensibility* and much of the juvenilia, proves that Austen disapproved of the behaviour these novels encouraged as well as the unrealistic expectations they promoted. It is possible then, that Jane intended her novels to serve in the same way, but with more suitable role models on offer. And such role models they have been! Austen's enduring popularity may not prove to be the intention of her work, but it is certainly a testament to the quality of her wit and wisdom.

Pictures of perfection as you know make me sick & wicked.

Letter to Fanny Knight, 23 March 1817

I do not want People to be very agreeable, as it saves me the trouble of liking them a great deal.

Letter to Cassandra Austen, 9 January 1799

Follies and nonsense, whims and inconsistencies, *do* divert me, I own, and I laugh at them whenever I can.

Pride and Prejudice

It was rather late in the day to set about being simple-minded and ignorant.

Emma

Now I must give one smirk, and then we may be rational again.

Northanger Abbey

Here I am once more in the Scene of Dissipation and vice, and I begin already to find my Morals corrupted.

Letter to Cassandra Austen, 23 August 1796

Business, you know, may bring you money, but friendship hardly ever does.

Emma

A large income is the best recipe for happiness I ever heard of.

Mansfield Park

People always live forever when there is an annuity to be paid them.

Sense and Sensibility

I am tolerably glad to hear that Edward's income is so good a one – as glad as I can at anybody's being rich besides You & me.

Letter to Cassandra, 9 January 1799

I must endeavour to subdue my mind to my fortune. I must learn to brook being happier than I deserve.

Persuasion

A very narrow income has the tendency to contract the mind, and sour the temper.

Emma

Happiness in marriage is entirely a matter of chance.

Pride and Prejudice

I wish you a merry Christmas, but *no* compliments of the Season.

Letter to Cassandra Austen, 9 January 1799

I am prevented from setting my black cap at Mr Maitland by his having a wife & ten children.

Letter to Cassandra Austen, 25 May 1801

I am very much obliged to Mrs Knight for such a proof of the interest she takes in me – & she may depend upon it, I *will* marry Mr Papillon, whatever his reluctance or my own. – I owe her much more than such a trifling sacrifice.

Letter to Cassandra Austen, 9 December 1808

Mrs. Jennings was a widow, with an ample jointure. She had only two daughters, both of whom she had lived to see respectably married, and she had now therefore nothing to do but marry all the rest of the world.

Sense and Sensibility

Mr Payne has been dead long enough for Henry to be out of mourning for him before his last visit, tho' we knew nothing of it till about that time. Why he died, or of what complaint, or to what Nobleman he bequeathed his four daughters in marriage we have not heard.

Letter to Cassandra Austen, 8 January 1801

What delight! what felicity! You give me fresh life and vigour. Adieu to disappointment and spleen. What are young men to rocks and mountains?

Pride and Prejudice

Nothing ever fatigues me but doing what I do not like.

Mansfield Park

There are people, who the more you do for them, the less they will do for themselves.

Emma

Such squeamish youths as cannot bear to be connected with a little absurdity are not worth a regret.

Pride and Prejudice

I bring back my heroine to her home in solitude and disgrace; and no sweet elation of spirits can lead me into minuteness. A heroine in a hack post-chaise is such a blow upon sentiment, as no attempt at grandeur or pathos can withstand.

Northanger Abbey

I always deserve the best treatment because I never put up with any other.

Emma

I had the comfort of finding out the other evening who all the fat girls with short noses were that disturbed me at the 1st H. Ball. They all prove to be Miss Atkinsons of Enham.

Letter to Cassandra Austen, 20 November 1800

An agreeable manner may set off handsome features, but can never alter plain ones.

Persuasion

Selfishness must always be forgiven, you know, because there is no hope of a cure.

Mansfield Park

It is very difficult for the prosperous to be humble.

Emma

How little permanent happiness of a couple who were only brought together because their passions were stronger than their virtue, she could easily conjecture.

Pride and Prejudice

People who have extensive grounds themselves are always pleased with any thing in the same style.

Emma

I will not say that your mulberry-trees are dead, but I am afraid they are not alive.

Letter to Cassandra Austen, 31 May 1811

One may be continually abusive without saying anything just; but one cannot always be laughing at a man without now and then stumbling on something witty.

Pride and Prejudice

She was of course only too good for him; but as nobody minds having what is too good for them, he was very steadily earnest in the pursuit of the blessing,

Mansfield Park

What a blessing it is, when undue influence does not survive the grave!

Emma

My dear little creature, do not stay at Portsmouth to lose your pretty looks. Those vile sea breezes are the ruin of beauty and health.

Mansfield Park

I must not depend upon being ever very blooming again. Sickness is a dangerous Indulgence at my time of Life.

Letter to Fanny Knight, 23 March 1817

Do not be frightened from the connection by your Brothers having most wit. Wisdom is better than Wit, & in the long run will certainly have the laugh on her side.

Letter to Fanny Knight, 18 November 1814

Seldom, very seldom, does complete truth belong to any human disclosure; seldom can it happen that something is not a little disguised, or a little mistaken.

Emma

Pride – where there is a real superiority of mind, pride will be always under good regulation.

Pride and Prejudice

With insufferable vanity had she believed herself in the secret of every body's feelings; with unpardonable arrogance proposed to arrange everybody's destiny.

Emma

Those who see quickly, will resolve quickly, and act quickly.

Mansfield Park

Nothing is more deceitful ... than the appearance of humility. It is often only carelessness of opinion, and sometimes an indirect boast.

Pride and Prejudice

I come home to be happy and indulgent.

Mansfield Park

Nothing amuses me more than the easy manner with which everybody settles the abundance of those who have a great deal less than themselves.

Mansfield Park

Vanity working on a weak head, produces every sort of mischief.

Emma

To be distinguished for elegance and accomplishments, the authorised object of their youth, could have had no useful influence that way, no moral effect on the mind.

Mansfield Park

Elinor honoured her for a plan which originated so nobly as this; though smiling to see the same eager fancy which had been leading her to the extreme of languid indolence and selfish repining, now at work in introducing excess into a scheme of such rational employment and virtuous self-control.

Sense and Sensibility

Vanity and pride are different things, though the words are often used synonymously. A person may be proud without being vain. Pride relates more to our opinion of ourselves, vanity to what we would have others think of us.

Pride and Prejudice

One half of the world cannot understand the pleasures of the other.

Emma

Every savage can dance.

Pride and Prejudice

Good-humoured, unaffected girls will not do for a man who has been used to sensible women. They are two distinct orders of being.

Mansfield Park

There is a meanness in *all* the arts which ladies sometimes condescend to employ for captivation. Whatever bears affinity to cunning is despicable.

Pride and Prejudice

Let your kindness defend what I know your judgment must censure.

Sense and Sensibility

A mind lively and at ease, can do with seeing nothing, can see nothing that does not answer.

Emma

I cannot speak well enough to be unintelligible.

Northanger Abbey

The power of doing anything with quickness is always prized much by the possessor, and often without any attention to the imperfection of the performance.

Pride and Prejudice

My protégé, as you call him, is a sensible man; and sense will always have attractions for me.

Sense and Sensibility

Do not speak ill of your Sense, merely for the Gratification of your Fancy. Yours is Sense, which deserves more honourable Treatment.

Letter to Fanny Knight, 20 February 1817

Silly things do cease to be silly if they are done by sensible people in an impudent way. Wickedness is always wickedness, but folly is not always folly.

Emma

There is nothing like employment, active indispensable employment, for relieving sorrow. Employment, even melancholy, may dispel melancholy, and her occupations were hopeful.

Mansfield Park

The pleasantness of an employment does not always evince its propriety.

Sense and Sensibility

Perfect happiness, even in memory, is not common.

Emma

We all love to instruct, though we can only teach what is not worth knowing.

Pride and Prejudice

Any real knowledge of a person's disposition that Bath, or any public place, can give – it is all nothing; there can be no knowledge. It is only by seeing women in their own homes, among their own set, just as they always are, that you can form any just judgment. Short of that, it is all guess and luck – and will generally be ill-luck.

Emma

I never meant to deceive you, but my spirits might often lead me wrong.

Pride and Prejudice

Can you trust me with such flatterers? Does my vain spirit ever tell me I am wrong?

Emma

I have courted prepossession and ignorance, and driven reason away, where either were concerned. Till this moment I never knew myself.

Pride and Prejudice

Know your own happiness. You want nothing but patience — or give it a more fascinating name, call it hope.

Sense and Sensibility

The indignities of stupidity, and the disappointments of selfish passion, can excite little pity.

Mansfield Park

A sanguine temper, though for ever expecting more good than occurs, does not always pay for its hopes by any proportionate depression. It soon flies over the present failure, and begins to hope again.

Emma

There is a stubbornness about me that never can bear to be frightened at the will of others. My courage always rises at every attempt to intimidate me.

Pride and Prejudice

Curiosity and vanity were both engaged, and the temptation of immediate pleasure was too strong for a mind unused to make any sacrifice to right.

Mansfield Park

You are the paragon of all that is Silly & Sensible, commonplace & eccentric, Sad & Lively, Provoking & Interesting.

Letter to Fanny Knight, 20 February 1817

'No, no,' cried Marianne, 'misery such as mine has no pride. I care not who knows that I am wretched. The triumph of seeing me so may be open to all the world. Elinor, Elinor, they who suffer little may be proud and independent as they like – may resist insult, or return mortification – but I cannot. I must feel – I must be wretched – and they are welcome to enjoy the consciousness of it that can.'

Sense and Sensibility

My temper I dare not vouch for. It is, I believe, too little yielding – certainly too little for the convenience of the world. I cannot forget the follies and vices of others so soon as I ought, nor their offences against myself. My feelings are not puffed about with every attempt to move them. My temper would perhaps be called resentful. My good opinion once lost, is lost forever.

Pride and Prejudice

If I was wrong in yielding to persuasion once, remember that it was to persuasion exerted on the side of safety, not of risk. When I yielded, I thought it was to duty; but no duty could be called in aid here. In marrying a man indifferent to me, all risk would have been incurred, and all duty violated.

Persuasion

There are few people whom I really love, and still fewer of whom I think well. The more I see of the world, the more I am dissatisfied with it; and every day confirms my belief of the inconsistency of all human characters, and of the little dependence that can be placed on the appearance of merit or sense.

Pride and Prejudice

You had made your own choice. It was not forced on you. Your wife has a claim to your politeness, to your respect, at least. She must be attached to you, or she would not have married you. To treat her with unkindness, to speak of her slightingly, is no atonement to Marianne; nor can I suppose it a relief to your own conscience.

Sense and Sensibility

If any one faculty of our nature may be called more wonderful than the rest, I do think it is memory. There seems
something more speakingly incomprehensible in the
powers, the failures, the inequalities of memory, than in
any other of our intelligences. The memory is sometimes
so retentive, so serviccable, so obedient; at others, so
bewildered and so weak; and at others again, so tyrannic,
so beyond control! We are, to be sure, a miracle every way;
but our powers of recollecting and of forgetting do seem
peculiarly past finding out.

Mansfield Park

You are all over Imagination. — The most astonishing part
of your Character is, that with so much Imagination, so
much flight of Mind, such unbounded Fancies, you should
have such excellent Judgement in what you do!

Letter to Fanny Knight, 13 March 1817

There will be little rubs and disappointments everywhere,
and we are all apt to expect too much; but then, if one
scheme of happiness fails, human nature turns to another;
if the first calculation is wrong, we make a second better:
we find comfort somewhere.

Mansfield Park

I considered the past; I saw in my own behaviour since the beginning of our acquaintance with him last autumn, nothing but a series of imprudence towards myself, and want of kindness to others. I saw that my own feelings had prepared my sufferings, and that my want of fortitude under them had almost led me to the grave. My illness, I well knew, had been entirely brought on by myself, by such negligence of my own health, as I had felt even at the time to be wrong.

Sense and Sensibility

Mr Darcy, I am a selfish creature; and, for the sake of giving relief to my own feelings, care not how much I may be wounding yours.

Pride and Prejudice

You frighten me out of my Wits by your reference. Your affection gives me the highest pleasure, but indeed you must not let anything depends on my opinion. Your own feelings & none but your own, should determine such an important point.

Letter to Fanny Knight, 30 November 1814

· 8 ·

POETRY

THOUGH JANE AUSTEN'S GREATEST gift was for prose, her pen was not unfamiliar with poetry. Both her mother and her brother James were talented poets and though Jane never found in verse the same genius she did in her novels, poems were sometimes penned in letters to her friends and family. Some are as playful and witty as her prose, whilst others give a more serious side to Austen's powers of observation. They are also honest and emotional in their sentiments too. 'Mock Panegyric on a Young Friend' is a sweet and playful praising of her beloved niece, Anna Austen, whilst 'To the Memory of Mrs. Lefroy who died Dec:r 16 – my Birthday' is an eloquent expression of grief. Anne Lefroy, aunt to the infamous Tom, was an important figure in Jane Austen's life at Steventon. She and her husband lived at the nearby Ashe Rectory and would have been close friends and neighbours with the Austen family. Jane admired the cultured, elegant Mrs Lefroy, who became something of a mentor to the budding writer.

Mock Panegyric on a Young Friend

In measured verse I'll now rehearse
The charms of lovely Anna:
And, first, her mind is unconfined
Like any vast savannah.

Ontario's lake may fitly speak
Her fancy's ample bound:
Its circuit may, on strict survey
Five hundred miles be found.

Her wit descends on foes and friends
Like famed Niagara's fall;
And travellers gaze in wild amaze,
And listen, one and all.

Her judgment sound, thick, black, profound,
Like transatlantic groves,
Dispenses aid, and friendly shade
To all that in it roves.

If thus her mind to be defined
America exhausts,
And all that's grand in that great land
In similes it costs —

Oh how can I her person try
To image and portray?
How paint the face, the form how trace,
In which those virtues lay?

Another world must be unfurled,
Another language known,
Ere tongue or sound can publish round
Her charms of flesh and bone.

My Dearest Frank, I wish you joy
My dearest Frank, I wish you joy
Of Mary's safety with a Boy,
Whose birth has given little pain
Compared with that of Mary Jane. —
May he a growing Blessing prove,
And well deserve his Parents' Love! —
Endow'd with Art's and Nature's Good,
Thy Name possessing with thy Blood,
In him, in all his ways, may we
Another Francis William see! —
Thy infant days may he inherit,
They warmth, nay insolence of spirit; —
We would not with one foult dispense
To weaken the resemblance.
May he revive thy Nursery sin,
Peeping as daringly within,
His curley Locks but just descried,
With 'Bet, my be not come to bide.'—
Fearless of danger, braving pain,
And threaten'd very oft in vain,
Still may one Terror daunt his Soul,
One needful engine of Controul
Be found in this sublime array,
A neighbouring Donkey's aweful Bray.
So may his equal faults as Child,
Produce Maturity as mild!
His saucy words and fiery ways
In early Childhood's pettish days,

In Manhood, shew his Father's mind
Like him, considerate and Kind;
All Gentleness to those around,
And anger only not to wound.
Then like his Father too, he must,
To his own former struggles just,
Feel his Deserts with honest Glow,
And all his self-improvement know.
A native fault may thus give birth
To the best blessing, conscious Worth.
As for ourselves we're very well;
As unaffected prose will tell. —
Cassandra's pen will paint our state,
The many comforts that await
Our Chawton home, how much we find
Already in it, to our mind;
And how convinced, that when complete
It will all other Houses beat
The ever have been made or mended,
With rooms concise, or rooms distended.
You'll find us very snug next year,
Perhaps with Charles and Fanny near,
For now it often does delight us
To fancy them just over-right us.

To the Memory of Mrs. Lefroy who died Dec:r 16 — my Birthday.

The day returns again, my natal day;
What mix'd emotions with the Thought arise!
Beloved friend, four years have pass'd away
Since thou wert snatch'd forever from our eyes. —
The day, commemorative of my birth
Bestowing Life and Light and Hope on me,
Brings back the hour which was thy last on Earth.
Oh! bitter pang of torturing Memory! —

Angelic Woman! past my power to praise
In Language meet, thy Talents, Temper, mind.
Thy solid Worth, they captivating Grace! —
Thou friend and ornament of Humankind! —

At Johnson's death by Hamilton t'was said,
'Seek we a substitute — Ah! vain the plan,
No second best remains to Johnson dead —
None can remind us even of the Man.'

So we of thee — unequall'd in thy race
Unequall'd thou, as he the first of Men.
Vainly we wearch around the vacant place,
We ne'er may look upon thy like again.

Come then fond Fancy, thou indulgant Power —
— Hope is desponding, chill, severe to thee! —
Bless thou, this little portion of an hour,
Let me behold her as she used to be.

I see her here, with all her smiles benign,
Her looks of eager Love, her accents sweet.
That voice and Countenance almost divine! –
Expression, Harmony, alike complete. –

I listen – 'tis not sound alone – 'tis sense,
'Tis Genius, Taste and Tenderness of Soul.
'Tis genuine warmth of heart without pretence
And purity of Mind that crowns the whole.

She speaks; 'tis Eloquence – that grace of Tongue
So rare, so lovely! – Never misapplied
By her to palliate Vice, or deck a Wrong,
She speaks and reasons but on Virtue's side.

Her's is the Energy of Soul sincere.
Her Christian Spirit ignorant to feign,
Seeks but to comfort, heal, enlighten, chear,
Confer a pleasure, or prevent a pain. –

Can ought enhance such Goodness? –Yes, to me,
Her partial favour from my earliest years
Consummates all. – Ah! Give me yet to see
Her smile of Love. – the Vision diappears.

'Tis past and gone –We meet no more below.
Short is the Cheat of Fancy o'er the Tomb.
Oh! might I hope to equal Bliss to go!
To meet thee Angel! in thy future home! –

Fain would I feel an union in thy fate,
Fain would I seek to draw an Omen fair
From this connection in our Earthly date.
Indulge the harmless weakness—Reason, spare. —

Happy the Lab'rer

Happy the lab'rer in his Sunday clothes!
In light-drab coat, smart waistcoat, well-darn'd hose,
And hat upon his head, to church he goes;
As oft, with conscious pride, he downward throws
A glance upon the ample cabbage rose
That, stuck in button-hole, regales his nose,
He envies not the gayest London beaux.
In church he takes his seat among the rows,
Pays to the place the reverence he owes,
Likes best the prayers whose meaning least he knows,
Lists to the sermon in a softening doze,
And rouses joyous at the welcome close.

Ode to Pity

1

Ever musing I delight to tread
The Paths of honour and the Myrtle Grove
Whilst the pale Moon her beams doth shed
On disappointed Love.
While Philomel on airy hawthorn Bush
Sings sweet and Melancholy, And the thrush
Converses with the Dove.

2

Gently brawling down the turnpike road,
Sweetly noisy falls the Silent Stream –
The Moon emerges from behind a Cloud
And darts upon the Myrtle Grove her beam.
Ah! then what Lovely Scenes appear,
The hut, the Cot, the Grot, and Chapel queer,
And eke the Abbey to a mouldering heap,
Conceal'd by aged pines her head doth rear
And quite invisible doth take a peep.

When Winchester races
When Winchester races first took their beginning
It is said the good people forgot their old Saint
Not applying at all for the leave of Saint Swithin
And that William of Wykeham's approval was faint.

The races however were fixed and determined
The company came and the Weather was charming
The Lords and the Ladies were satine'd and ermined
And nobody saw any future alarming. –

But when the old Saint was informed of these doings
He made but one Spring from his Shrine to the Roof
Of the Palace which now lies so sadly in ruins
And then he addressed them all standing aloof.

'Oh! subjects rebellious! Oh Venta depraved
When once we are buried you think we are gone

But behold me immortal! By vice you're enslaved
You have sinned and must suffer, ten farther he said

These races and revels and dissolute measures
With which you're debasing a neighbouring Plain
Let them stand – You shall meet with your curse in your
pleasures
Set off for your course, I'll pursue with my rain.

Ye cannot but know my command o'er July
Henceforward I'll triumph in shewing my powers
Shift your race as you will it shall never be dry
The curse upon Venta is July in showers –'.

Of A Ministry Pitiful, Angry, Mean
Of a Ministry pitiful, angry, mean,
A gallant commander the victim is seen.
For promptitude, vigour, success, does he stand
Condemn'd to receive a severe reprimand!
To his foes I could wish a resemblance in fate:
That they, too, may suffer themselves, soon or late,
The injustice they warrent. But vain is my spite
They cannot so suffer who never do right.

This Little Bag
This little bag I hope will prove
To be not vainly made –
For, if you should a needle want
It will afford you aid.
And as we are about to part
T'will serve another end,
For when you look upon the Bag
You'll recollect your friend

When Stretch'd on One's Bed
When stretch'd on one's bed
With a fierce-throbbing head,
Which precludes alike thought or repose,
How little one cares
For the grandest affairs
That may busy the world as it goes!

How little one feels
For the waltzes and reels
Of our Dance-loving friends at a Ball!
How slight one's concern
To conjecture or learn
What their flounces or hearts may befall.

How little one minds
If a company dines
On the best that the Season affords!
How short is one's muse

O'er the Sauces and Stews,
Or the Guests, be they Beggars or Lords.

How little the Bells,
Ring they Peels, toll they Knells,
Can attract our attention or Ears!
The Bride may be married,
The Corse may be carried
And touch nor our hopes nor our fears.

Our own bodily pains
Ev'ry faculty chains;
We can feel on no subject besides.
'Tis in health and in ease
We the power must seize
For our friends and our souls to provide.

ON AUSTEN

Since her first publication in 1811, Jane Austen has been something of a hot topic amongst her contemporaries and critics. Some have adored her; Sir Walter Scot expressed himself as a great admirer of her work – just as she had once done for his. Her novels even gained royal attention, not just from the Prince Regent but from his daughter Princess Charlotte who was pleased by the romantic, impulsive Marianne Dashwood. However, not all that has been said on Austen has been entirely complimentary. When George Eliot's partner, the philosopher and critic G.H Lewes, wrote of his appreciation of Austen's work to his friend Charlotte Brontë, she replied that she could not understand why. The author of *Jane Eyre* found Austen's intricately detailed, carefully constructed world too cold and without passion for her tastes. Mark Twain was equally unimpressed with Austen, and once commented that any good library must be one without her work in it.

The calm surface world of Austen's novels may not have always been well received, but beneath the neat exterior is Austen's genius. Her characters are complex and her

Cassandra's watercolour of Jane. (*c.* 1810)

understanding of human nature almost omniscient. Though public opinion continues to shift when it comes to Austen – for some her work is a classic romance, for others satirical brilliance and yes, some find it lacking – her fame has far from waned. Jane Austen, it seems, will always be a name that is spoken across the world.

Her power of inventing characters seems to have been intuitive, and almost unlimited. She drew from nature; but, whatever may have been surmised to the contrary, never from individuals. The style of her familiar correspondence was in all respects the same as that of her novels. Every thing came finished from her pen; for on all subjects she had ideas as clear as her expressions were well chosen. It is not hazarding too much to say that she never dispatched a note or letter unworthy of publication.

Henry Austen, from a 'Biographical Notice of the Author'

I have lost a treasure, such a sister, such a friend as never can have been surpassed. She was the sun of my life, the gilder of every pleasure, the soother of every sorrow; I had not a thought concealed from her, and it is as if I had lost a part of myself. I loved her only too well – not better than she deserved, but I am conscious that my affection for her made me sometimes unjust to and negligent of others; and I can acknowledge, more than as a general principle, the justice of the Hand which has struck this blow.

Cassandra Austen, in a letter to Fanny Knight, 1817

On such Subjects, no Wonder that she should write well
In whom so united those Qualities dwell;
Where dear Sensibility, Sterne's darling Maid,
With Sense so attemper'd is finely portray'd.
Fair Elinor's self in that Mind is exprest,
And the feelings of Marianne live in that Breast.
Oh then, gentle Lady! continue to write,
And the Sense of your Readers t'amuse and delight.

> 'To Miss Jane Austen, reputed author of Sense and
> Sensibility, a Novel lately published' by James Austen

No words can express, my dear Aunt, my surprise
Or make you conceive how I opened my eyes,
Like a pig Butcher Pile has just struck with his knife,
When I heard for the very first time in my life
That I had the honour to have a relation
Whose works were dispersed throughout the whole of
the nation.
I assure you, however, I'm terribly glad;
Oh dear! just to think (and the thought drives me mad)
That you made the Middletons, Dashwoods, and all,
And that you (not young Ferrars) found out that a ball
May be given in cottages never so small.
And though Mr. Collins, so grateful for all,
Will Lady de Bourgh his dear Patroness call,
'Tis to your ingenuity he really owed
His living, his wife, and his humble abode.

> James Edward Austen Leigh, in a letter to
> Jane Austen, 1813

In her, rare union, were combined a fair form, and a fairer mind;

Hers fancy quick, and clear good sense,

And wit which never gave offence;

A heart as warm as ever beat, A temper even; calm & sweet.

Though quick & keen her mental eye Poor nature's foibles to espy,

And seemed forever on the watch,

Some trails of ridicule to catch

Yet not a word she ever penned

Which hurt the feelings of a friend.

And not one line she ever wrote

Which dying she would wish to blot;

But to her family alone

Her real, genuine worth was known.

James Austen, published posthumously

In Memory of JANE AUSTEN, youngest daughter of the late Revd GEORGE AUSTEN, formerly Rector of Steventon in this County. She departed this Life on the 18th of July 1817, aged 41, after a long illness supported with the patience and the hopes of a Christian. The benevolence of her heart, the sweetness of her temper, and the extraordinary endowments of her mind obtained the regard of all who knew her and the warmest love of her intimate connections. Their grief is in proportion to their affection, they know their loss to be irreparable, but in their deepest affliction they are consoled by a firm though humble hope that her charity, devotion, faith and purity have rendered her soul acceptable in the sight of her REDEEMER.

Inscription on Jane Austen's gravestone, Winchester Cathedral

Yes my love it is very true that Aunt Jane from various circumstances was not so refined as she ought to have been from her talent, and if she had lived fifty years later she would have been in many respects more suitable to our more refined tastes. They were not rich & the people around with whom they chiefly mixed, were not at all high bred, or in short anything more than mediocre & they of course tho' superior in mental powers & cultivation were on the same level as far as refinement goes – but I think in later life their intercourse with Mrs. Knight (who was very fond & kind to them) improved them both & Aunt Jane was too clever not to put aside all possible signs of 'common-ness' (if such an expression is allowable) & teach herself to be more refined at least in intercourse with people in general.

Letter from Lady Fanny Knatchbull, previously Austen Knight, to her sister Marianne, 1869

Austen is to Shakespeare as asteroid to sun. Miss Austen's novels are perfect works on small scale – beautiful bits of stippling.

Alfred, Lord Tennyson

I have finished the Novel called *Pride and Prejudice*, which I think a very superior work. It depends not on any of the common resources of novel writers, no drownings, no conflagrations, nor runaway horses, nor lap-dogs and parrots, nor chambermaids and milliners, nor rencontres [duels] and disguises. I really think it is the most probable I have ever read. It is not a crying book, but the interest is very strong, especially for Mr Darcy. The characters which are not amiable are diverting, and all of them are consistently supported.

Anabella Milbanke, later Lady Byron, in a letter to her
mother, 1813

I often want to criticize Jane Austen, but her books madden me so that I can't conceal my frenzy from the reader; and therefore I have to stop every time I begin. Every time I read 'Pride and Prejudice' I want to dig her up and beat her over the skull with her own shin-bone.

Mark Twain

Jane's Marriage

JANE went to Paradise:
That was only fair.
Good Sir Walter met her first,
And led her up the stair.
Henry and Tobias,
And Miguel of Spain,
Stood with Shakespeare at the top
To welcome Jane –
Then the Three Archangels
Offered out of hand,
Anything in Heaven's gift
That she might command.
Azrael's eyes upon her,
Raphael's wings above,
Michael's sword against her heart,
Jane said: 'Love.'
Instantly the under-
standing Seraphim
Laid their fingers on their lips
And went to look for him.
Stole across the Zodiac,
Harnessed Charles's Wain,
And whispered round the Nebulae
'Who loved Jane?'
In a private limbo
Where none had thought to look,
Sat a Hampshire gentleman
Reading of a book.

It was called *Persuasion*,
And it told the plain
Story of the love between
Him and Jane.
He heard the question
Circle Heaven through –
Closed the book and answered:
'I did – and do!'
Quietly but speedily
(As Captain Wentworth moved)
Entered into Paradise
The man Jane loved!

Rudyard Kipling

First and foremost let Jane Austen be named, the greatest artist that has ever written, using the term to signify the most perfect mastery over the means to her end. There are heights and depths in human nature Miss Austen has never scaled nor fathomed, there are worlds of passionate existence into which she has never set foot; but although this is obvious to every reader, it is equally obvious that she risked no failures by attempting to delineate that which she had not seen. Her circle may be restricted, but it is complete. Her world is a perfect orb, and vital.

G.H. Lewes, in *The Lady Novelists*, 1852

Jane lies in Winchester – blessed be her shade!
Praise the Lord for making her, and her for all she made!
And while the stones of Winchester, or Milsom Street, remain,
Glory, love, and honour unto England's Jane!

> Rudyard Kipling, in the poem 'Jane's Marriage' in *The
> Janeites*, 1926

I am a Jane Austenite, and therefore slightly imbecile about
Jane Austen. My fatuous expression, and airs of personal
immunity – how ill they sit on the face, say, of a Stevensonian!
But Jane Austen is so different. She is my favourite author! I
read and reread, the mouth open and the mind closed. Shut
up in measureless content, I greet her by the name of most
kind hostess, while criticism slumbers.

> E.M. Forster, in *Waking the Jane Austenite up*, 1924

Why do you like Miss Austen so very much? I am puzzled
on that point. What induced you to say that you would
have rather written 'Pride and Prejudice' or 'Tom Jones',
than any of the Waverley Novels? I had not seen 'Pride and
Prejudice' till I read that sentence of yours, and then I got
the book. And what did I find? An accurate daguerreotyped
portrait of a commonplace face; a carefully fenced, highly
cultivated garden, with neat borders and delicate flowers;
but no glance of a bright, vivid physiognomy, no open country, no fresh air, no blue hill, no bonny beck. I should hardly
like to live with her ladies and gentlemen, in their elegant
but confined houses.

> Charlotte Brontë, in a letter to G.H. Lewes, 1848

Sence and Sencibility [sic] I have just finished read-ing; it certainly is interesting, & you feel quite one of the company. I think Maryanne [sic] & me are very like in disposition, that certainly I am not so good, the same imprudence, &, however remain very like. I must say it interested me much.

Princess Charlotte, daughter of the Prince Regent, in a letter to a friend

One does not read Jane Austen, one re-reads Jane Austen.

W.F Buckley Jnr

Also read again, and for the third time at least, Miss Austen's very finely written novel of *Pride and Prejudice*. That young lady had a talent for describing the involve-ment and feelings and characters of ordinary life which is to me the most wonderful I ever met with. The big Bow-wow strain I can do myself like any now going, but the exquisite touch which renders ordinary commonplace things and characters interesting from the truth of the description and the sentiment is denied to me. What a pity such a gifted creature died so early!

Sir Walter Scott, in his diary entry for 14 March 1826

Miss Austen was surely a great novelist. What she did, she did perfectly. Her work, as far as it goes, is faultless. She wrote of the times in which she lived, of the class of people with which she associated, and in the language which was usual to her as an educated lady. Of romance, – what we generally mean when we speak of romance – she had no tinge. Heroes and heroines with wonderful adventures there are none in her novels. Of great criminals and hidden crimes she tells us nothing. But she places us in a circle of gentlemen and ladies, and charms us while she tells us with an unconscious accuracy how men should act to women, and women act to men. It is not that her people are all good; – and, certainly, they are not all wise. The faults of some are the anvils on which the virtues of others are hammered till they are bright as steel. In the comedy of folly I know no novelist who has beaten her.

Anthony Trollope, 1870